MATTHEW BOULTON
and the Art of Making Money

MATTHEW BOULTON
and the Art of Making Money

Edited by Richard Clay and Sue Tungate

BREWIN BOOKS

First published by
Brewin Books Ltd, 56 Alcester Road,
Studley, Warwickshire B80 7LG in 2009
www.brewinbooks.com

ISBN: 978-1-85858-450-8

A Cataloguing in Publication Record
for this title is available from the British Library.

Typeset in Baskerville
Printed in Great Britain by
Hobbs the Printers Ltd.

Contents

Acknowledgements

The curatorial team of the Barber Institute of Fine Arts exhibition *Matthew Boulton and the Art of Making Money* offer sincere thanks to: the Henry Moore Foundation and the University of Birmingham's 'Deans Special Initiative Fund' whose financial support made the publication of this catalogue possible; Dr Eurydice Georganteli who, as the Barber Institute's Keeper of Coins, supported the development of this exhibition, helped negotiate loans and funding, and offered invaluable guidance; the staff of the British Museum who installed the exhibition with consummate skill and generously gave crucial advice throughout the project; the staff of The Birmingham Assay Office, especially Dr Sally Baggott, and of the Birmingham Museums and Art Galleries who facilitated their institutions' large loans to the exhibition and who so kindly shared their great academic and curatorial expertise; the staff of the Barber Institute who made the exhibition a reality (especially: Sarah Brown, Andrew Davies, Yvonne Locke, Rosemary Poynton, Paul Spencer-Longhurst, Jonathan Shea, John Van Boolen, and Sophie Wilson); the Arts and Humanities Research Council whose grant money supported a workshop series (*Investigating and Communicating the Historical Significance of Matthew Boulton [1728-1809]*) that informed the exhibition's development; David Vice who allowed reference to be made to his unpublished work in this catalogue's chapters by Richard Clay, David Symons, and Sue Tungate.

Those members of the curatorial team who have contributed writings to this catalogue would like to offer special thanks to Val Loggie (AHRC Collaborative PhD student, University of Birmingham, and Birmingham Museums and Art Galleries) for the crucial role she played in the exhibition's development.

Professor Ann Sumner,
Director of the Barber Institute of Fine Arts

Introduction

Matthew Boulton and the art of making money[1]

Sue Tungate

The Barber Institute of Fine Arts exhibition, *Matthew Boulton and the art of making money*, commemorates the 2009 bicentenary of the death of Matthew Boulton (1728-1809). The exhibition was made possible by generous loans from the collections of the Birmingham Assay Office, the British Museum, Birmingham Museums and Art Gallery, and two private collectors. The objects on display show the astonishing range of fine quality coins, medals and tokens produced at Matthew Boulton's Soho Mint between 1789 and 1809.[2] The mint's international team mastered the mechanical and liberal arts that made it possible to make money on a massive scale and, in the process, Boulton made money in a less literal sense by turning a profit.

Matthew Boulton was a Birmingham entrepreneur, manufacturer, engineer, and scientist; a man with wide interests and an enormous network of contacts across the world. He is often referred to as the 'Father of Birmingham' and, apart from his manufacturing businesses at Soho, Boulton campaigned for the establishment of the Birmingham Assay Office in 1773,[3] helped develop the theatre in New Street in 1774, contributed to the founding of the town's General Hospital and a Library in 1779,[4] and he was involved in the extension of the canal

1   This chapter is based on work that the author is conducting as part of her Arts and Humanities Research Council-funded collaborative PhD under the supervision of staff at the University of Birmingham and at Birmingham Museums and Art Gallery.
    All MS manuscript references are from the Birmingham Central Library's Archives of Soho.
2   There were at least three Mints at Soho, the third of which was established after Boulton's death in 1809. But, with the exception of memorial medals, only Soho pieces produced up until Boulton's death are included in the exhibition which this catalogue accompanies.
3   Chris Upton, *A History of Birmingham*, Chichester, 1997, p.70.
4   Richard Doty, *The Soho Mint and the Industrialisation of Money,* British Numismatic Society Special Publication, no. 2, London, 1998, p.10.

system to Birmingham. Boulton chaired Birmingham's General Chamber of Manufacturers in 1785, and the town's Commercial Committee in 1787,[5] he worked with Birmingham's Street Commissioners, acted as Sheriff of Staffordshire in 1794,[6] and was involved in the work of various government committees.[7] He was a co-founder of the Lunar Society,[8] whose members included: Josiah Wedgwood, Erasmus Darwin (grandfather of Charles), James Keir, William Withering, and Joseph Priestley. Boulton was made a Fellow of the Royal Society of Edinburgh in 1784 and of the Royal Society in November 1785.[9] His wide-ranging business and personal letters, diaries, and notebooks provide a unique record of eighteenth-century life.[10]

The Soho Mint was part of Matthew Boulton's extensive metal manufacturing business from 1789 onward. He had started his commercial enterprises by making buttons and buckles in Birmingham, working with his father during the 1740s and 1750s. From 1761 he began the construction of his Soho Manufactory just outside of Birmingham. During his lifetime it became one of the most famous industrial sites in the world, renowned as a centre of excellence in metal working. The ormolu, silverware and other goods produced there greatly influenced taste and fashion of the period, and helped raise the reputation of goods produced in Birmingham. Boulton's workers were skilled craftsmen, well paid, and equipped with all manner of labour-saving devices. His team developed ingenious designs that enabled many of their beautiful products to be assembled from relatively small numbers of components, each of which was manufactured in quantity.[11] By 1765, Boulton had

---

5   *Morning Herald & Daily Advertiser,* 13 June 1785; *Gazetter & New Daily Advertiser*, 6 April 1787, Issue 18197.

6   Boulton was also nominated in 1792. He had been nominated as Sheriff of Warwickshire in 1789. *Argus,* 16 November 1789, Issue 217; *General Evening Post,* 10 November 1792, Issue 9226; *Morning Chronicle*, 10 February 1794.

7   For example, he had met with William Pitt in February 1785 for discussions about iron and trade and taxes. AD1583/1/47 10 Feb 1785 Boulton to Wilson. From Cornish Mining Heritage: Wilson Papers available at http://www.cornish-mining.org.uk/story/bwpapers. htm.

8   Details on the members of the Lunar Society can be found at http://www.revolutionaryplayers.org.uk.

9   Boulton was elected to the Royal Society on 24 November 1785. James Watt was elected a Fellow on the same date. The Royal Society Repository GB 117, Reference Number EC/1785/12.

10   Boulton's business and personal records are housed in the Archives of Soho at Birmingham Reference Library. Both sides of the correspondence are often available due to the use of James Watt's letter copying machine. For details of this Archive see: Fiona Tait, *How do we know what we know? The Archives of Soho* in Shena Mason (ed), *Matthew Boulton: Selling What all the World Desires*, London and New Haven, 2009.

11   Boulton also produced steel toys, patent latchets, rolled metal, steam engines, pneumatic apparatus, and copying machines in a variety of firms set up by 1798.

brought all the functions of a modern business, including research, design and marketing, under his control at Soho, and his products were being sold all over Europe.[12]

Boulton was an excellent entrepreneur, but he also oversaw and conducted research into industrial processes, contributing to the development of new technologies. In the 1770s he played a key role in making James Watt's condensing steam engine design a reality, providing the finance, the skilled workmen and the drive to extend Watt's original patent until 1799 (**Fig 1**). Boulton suggested to Watt some of the most important developments in the steam engine's design, and he had a keen appreciation of the commercial opportunities offered by an engine that could produce a constant

Fig 1. Reverse, copper medal Watts steam engine, 1819 (Assay Office 272) (Reproduced courtesy of The Birmingham Assay Office).

rotary motion.[13] Importantly, Boulton saw that such steam power could be harnessed to solve the problems posed by Britain's serious shortage of small change.

The Royal Mint in London traditionally held a monopoly on making coins – those pieces of metal that the government had authorized for use as legal tender. Originally, regal coins had contained metal worth as much as the object's ostensible value (for example, a penny was made of a penny's worth of metal). But, as David Symons shows in his chapter in this catalogue, during the eighteenth century, counterfeiting of regal coins was rampant in Britain, and Boulton, like many of his contemporaries, was concerned that workmen were being cheated when they were paid with counterfeit coins. Boulton believed that he could produce sufficient coinage to supply the needs of the growing industrial workforce, and that he could do it more cheaply than the Royal Mint. Furthermore, Boulton stood to make a profit from such an endeavour by using up surpluses of copper produced by the Cornish mines where many of Boulton and Watt's steam engines were employed. But producing coins was not a simple matter.

---

12 A letter from Fothergill to Boulton in 1764 lists the merchants handling their goods in Germany, America, Spain, Russia, Italy, Holland, Sweden, and Britain. Goodison lists the patrons that Boulton had cultivated by 1778, including: ambassadors and visitors from America, Austria, Denmark, France, Germany, Italy, Netherlands, Poland, Portugal, Russia, Sardinia, Spain, Sweden and Switzerland. Nicholas Goodison, *Matthew Boulton Ormolu*, London, 2002, pp.404-406.

13 Many instances of technical improvements concerning the steam engine and the mint are found in Boulton's correspondence with Watt. Indeed, in 1783 Boulton discussed reports of him being credited with its invention alongside Watt. MS 3147-3-7-7, 16 April 1783, Matthew Boulton (London) to James Watt (Birmingham).

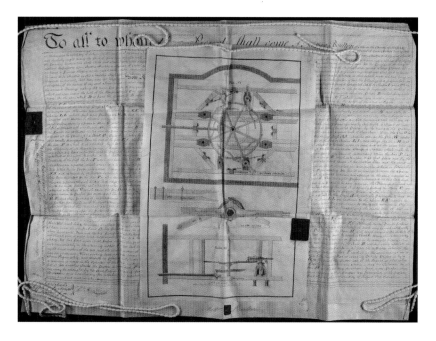

Fig 2. Coining press patent diagram, *ink on paper, 1790 (Soho Archives, MS 3782-17-2a) (Reproduced courtesy of Birmingham Libraries and Archives).*

In order to establish a successful mint, Boulton had to obtain metal of a suitable quantity and quality, develop the technology and build the equipment needed, and recruit and train suitable workers (including: engineers, workmen, designers, engravers, and salesmen). The metal had to go through the processes of rolling, annealing, blank cutting, edge marking and striking. Coins then had to be finished, polished, packed, and distributed to places that, as Boulton's business expanded, were as far apart as North America, Africa, Australia, Europe, India and Sumatra. Nevertheless, by 1789, following many experiments, Boulton's team of engineers had built the world's first steam powered mint at Soho (**Fig 2**).[14] Each

---

14 1790 Coining Press Patent, MS 3782-17-2a The first steam-powered coining press worked by a sliding rod connected, via an air pump, to the condenser of the steam engine. But by 1789 a connection to a horizontal flywheel raised the screw of the coining press as it turned. The power for the blow of the die on the blank was given initially by releasing weights which dropped when a pin on the flywheel disconnected. But soon air pumps replaced the weights and, eventually, eight coining presses in a circle were run by this machine that was patented in 1790. In 1798, after Boulton's first regal coinage order, the horizontal fly wheel was replaced by reciprocating engines working each press individually by means of a partial vacuum. See Peter Jones' chapter in this book for a discussion of the second mint at Soho.

of its new coin presses eventually had an automatic layer-in which fed the blanks (plain circles of metal) between dies that were engraved with reversed versions of the imagery and lettering. The dies, attached to a steam-driven screw press, were then forced onto the blank, impressing the blank's sides and edges with the design. The finished coin was then removed automatically and an air pump provided the return stroke of the engine, ensuring that the whole mechanical process of minting could be rapidly repeated.

Boulton was involved in every aspect of the Soho Mint's development, giving detailed instructions on how the rooms should be arranged, how the metal should be rolled and cleaned, and how the dies should be forged and engraved.[15] He introduced new techniques in die making, such as the use of a ring shaped die which enabled the Soho Mint to produce more uniform coins than had ever been made before. His great knowledge of the mechanical and metallurgical arts, his leadership, and his determination were recognized at the time by his co-workers.

> That the management & methodizing of the whole was exclusively [Boulton's] own; & that to his indefatigable energy & perseverance in pursuit of this the favourite & nearly the sole object of the last twenty years of the active part of his life is to be attributed the perfection it has ultimately attained.[16]

Boulton's development of a motivated workforce was crucial to the Soho Mint's eventual success. He already had experienced assistants such as James Lawson, who had worked for him erecting steam engines in Cornwall, John Southern, and his own son, Matthew Robinson Boulton. The existing Soho Rolling Mill, run by John Kellet, was able to expand to roll for the mint and, on site, there were specialists in die forging, cutting, and annealing – John Busch, John Peploe and Joseph Harrison.[17] The mint's team also included Boulton's London bankers, William and Charlotte Matthews, and a series of talented engravers, including those recruited from overseas, such as Jean-Pierre Droz, Conrad Heinrich Küchler, Rambert Dumarest, and Noel-Alexandre Ponthon, as well as local talent such as John Gregory Hancock, Thomas Wyon, and John Phillp.

In 1787 Boulton was involved in a campaign to persuade the British Government to commission a large issue of small denomination regal coinage,

---

15   For example, see a list of 18 resolutions about the Mint arrangements. MS 3782-13-36 Item 54, 26 May 1791. Matthew Boulton to Matthew Robinson Boulton.

16   MS 3782-13-120, Minutes of a meeting held at Soho on 7 January 1810 with James Watt, William Murdoch, James Lawson, John Southern, Peter Ewart, and Matthew Robinson Boulton.

17   MS 3782-12-108, Item 53, Mint Notebook, 1788, p.10 and p.52.

using up to 3000 tons of copper. In February 1788, Boulton believed that he had been granted permission to go ahead with production. Hence, he started to build his mint in his back garden at Soho.[18] But, as David Symons, Peter Jones, and Richard Clay discuss in their chapters in this catalogue, Boulton did not actually win the contract to produce regal coin until 1797. In the meantime, he had a fully functioning mint and, as Peter Jones shows, Boulton used it to mint unofficial money for, among others, the Monneron Brothers in Paris. Richard Clay discusses how, in Britain, the lack of regal coin led private individuals to commission their own issues of small change in the form of tokens that bore a promise of repayment in regal coin or goods. Such tokens were distributed from 1787 onwards by industrial leaders who issued heavy, well made copper penny or halfpenny tokens, initially made in Birmingham by John Westwood, but later often made by Matthew Boulton at Soho.

The exhibition that this catalogue accompanies includes examples of tokens produced for circulation across Britain and Ireland, including those used at the Irish Cronebane Mine – the first in the world to be coined by steam-powered presses. Also on display are tokens made at Soho for other mining companies, including those in Anglesey and Cornwall, for iron manufactures like John Wilkinson, and for merchants in towns such as Leeds, Glasgow, Bishop's Stortford, Lancaster, Birmingham, and Nottingham. In addition, Soho produced tokens for aristocrats, such as Viscount Charleville, and for entrepreneurs, such as Isaac Swainson and Christopher Ibberson (advertising Vegetable Syrup and coaching services, respectively). Boulton also made numerous medals which are indicative of the growing emphasis on notions of meritocracy in late eighteenth-century Britain. Such objects were commissioned by local military groups in Nottingham, Manchester and Birmingham, for Friendly Societies at Hafod and St Albans, and for the Society of Arts and the Board of Agriculture. The astonishingly diverse designs of the tokens and medals made at Soho for domestic consumption offer a highly valuable resource for the study of eighteenth-century British society. Such objects offer us fascinating insights into British people's senses of regional, national, and trade identity.

While Boulton continued to pursue the elusive regal coining contract during the 1790s, his most important minting work, in terms of numbers and longevity, came from the Honourable East India Company for which Soho made coins in enormous quantities; for example, 17 million coins in 1791 for Bombay, and 13 million coins for Madras in 1794. The Soho Mint also produced pattern coins for Russia and

---

18   MS 3782-13-36, Item 19, 8 February 1788, Matthew Boulton (London) to Matthew Robinson
     Boulton (Paris).

Denmark and this work eventually led to Boulton supplying these countries with entire mints. Furthermore, Soho sold presses and blanks to the Philadelphia Mint in the USA from 1792.[19] In 1797, when Boulton was finally commissioned to provide a new regal coinage for Britain, Soho produced 480 tons of the famous 'Cartwheel pennies' (43,969,204 coins), and 20 tons of two pence pieces. In 1799 over 46 million halfpennies and farthings were issued, using 550 tons of copper. Between 1806 and 1807, Boulton's team went on to make over 165 million regal coins in fifteen months.[20] Yet, even once Boulton had begun to mint small change for the British Government, Soho continued to produce coins for overseas. Between 1802 and 1804 more than 66 million coins were sent from Soho to St Botolph's wharf in London to be loaded onto the East India Company's ships ready for delivery to the Indian subcontinent. By the time of Boulton's death in 1809, the Soho Mint had produced coins, medals and tokens for around twenty countries, using at least ten languages. By mastering the 'art of making money', the Soho Mint's team, built by Boulton, had played a crucial role in oiling the wheels of the emerging global cash economy.

In a letter that he wrote in 1802, Boulton emphasised the practical rather than the aesthetic priorities of his coining activities, arguing that

> The most important improvement to be desired in ye art of Moneying is not in making beautiful specimens but in making such Money as cannot be counterfeited with Profit to the Culprit, by such means as will produce a million of pieces per day if necessary, at a small expense.[21]

Yet, there can be little doubt that 'beautiful specimens' were also important to Boulton, he had gone to great lengths to secure the services of the highest quality designers and engravers. Indeed, by the time he wrote the aforementioned letter, he had been credited by Stebbing Shaw with reviving 'that branch of sculpture, which has been upon the decline in this kingdom since the death of Symons in the reign of Charles II'.[22] As Richard Clay argues in his chapter in this catalogue, the Soho Mint's

---

19 After Boulton's death coins were made at the Soho Mint for Argentina, Mexico, Brazil, Chile, Singapore, St Helena, Australia, Canada and Guernsey, and mints were supplied to Calcutta and South America.

20 It may seem surprising that exact numbers can be given for the production of coins, medals, and tokens. However, it is possible to find these figures in the Archives of Soho, in Mint record books, invoices and so on. Thanks are due to David Vice who kindly allowed me to use the numbers detailed in his forthcoming publication: D. Vice, 'A numismatic history of Soho Manufactory and Mint 1772-1850', *British Numismatic Journal*.

21 MS 3782-12-75, 1 November 1802, Matthew Boulton (Soho) to Zaccheus Walker Jr. (Paris).

22 Stebbing Shaw, *The History and Antiquities of Staffordshire*, Volume II, Part I, Wakefield, 1976 (facsimile of the original text published 1798-1801), p.119.

coins, medals, and tokens put the products of the liberal as well as the mechanical arts into the hands of millions of people across the world of all social classes. Furthermore, the Soho Mint's products encouraged the surging interest in collecting coins, medals, and tokens in late eighteenth-century and early nineteenth-century Britain.[23] While copper tokens were accessible to collectors who were not especially wealthy, the social elite also collected the more expensive medals produced at the Soho Mint. Indeed, some of the medals on display in this exhibition were owned originally by George III. Long before coins and tokens were produced at Soho, medals had been fashioned there as part of Boulton's 'toy' trade – they were issued to celebrate events and personalities. Making use of the outstanding engravers working at Soho, Boulton produced a series of beautiful medals, usually in runs of no more than 500, and in a huge variety of designs.[24] Some were made on commission, but others on a speculative basis.

The products of the Soho Mint were among Matthew Boulton's greatest achievements. The efficiency of Soho's automated steam-driven presses enabled huge quantities of coins, medals, and tokens to be made cheaply – nearly 600 million of them by the time of Boulton's death in 1809. But the improved die-making and metal rolling technologies developed at Soho, along with the use of highly skilled engravers, meant that quality was not compromised in favour of quantity. It seems fitting that the final words in this catalogue's introduction should be those of James Watt who wrote, in Matthew Boulton's obituary, that

Had Mr B done nothing more in the world than what he has done in improving the coinage, his fame would have deserved to be immortalised; and if it is considered that this was done in the midst of various other important avocations, & at an enormous expense for which he could have no certainty of an adequate return, we shall be at a loss as to whether to admire most his ingenuity, his perseverance or his munificence.[25]

---

23   It is clearly the case that many different token designs were produced by other manufacturers in very small numbers and that they were aimed only at the collectors market. Dalton and Hamer have identified at least seven thousand varieties. R. Dalton and S. H. Hamer, *The Provincial Token-Coinage of the Eighteenth Century Illustrated*, Bristol, 1910.

24   An exception being the 14,000 Trafalgar medals made in 1806 at Soho Mint at Boulton's own expense to give to those who had participated in the battle.

25   H.W. Dickinson, *Matthew Boulton*, Cambridge, 1937, p.205. Quotation from James Watt's Memorial to Matthew Boulton written on 17 September 1809.

Chapter One

Matthew Boulton and the forgers

David Symons

One of the main arguments that Matthew Boulton always advanced in favour of reforming the British copper coinage was the need to put an end to the epidemic of forgery which afflicted the currency in the later eighteenth century. To understand fully Boulton's motivation, we need first to examine in some detail the situation that he and his contemporaries faced.

The state of Britain's copper coinage in the later eighteenth century was generally deplorable. Comparatively little copper coin had been struck by the Royal Mint since 1754, with just a small issue in 1762-3, a rather larger amount in 1770-5 **(Fig 3a)**, and none at all for more than two decades after that.[1] Since this was just the time that the growth of industrialisation was creating a workforce that depended on small change to buy its everyday necessities, the limited production of copper coins was a major problem. Even worse, what copper coins the Royal Mint did produce could only be acquired at the Mint itself, in the Tower of London, and the purchaser then had to bear the cost of shipping them where they were required. The natural result

Fig 3a. Obverse (top) and reverse (bottom), copper halfpenny, 1771, in the condition it entered circulation (BMAG 1969 N 602).

---

1   Sir John Craig, *The Mint. A History of the London Mint from A.D. 287 to 1948*, Cambridge, 1953, p.251; see P. Dyer and P.P. Gaspar, 'Reform, the new technology and Tower Hill, 1700-1966', in C.E. Challis (ed.), *A New History of the Royal Mint*, Cambridge, 1992, p.436 for a table giving the Royal Mint's output of copper coins. To be fair to the Mint, it was the government that decided when copper coins should be struck and how many should be produced, not the Mint itself. G. Selgin, *Good Money. Birmingham Button Makers, the Royal Mint, and the Beginnings of Modern Coinage, 1775-1821. Private Enterprise and Popular Coinage*, Oakland (California), 2008, p.20, p.22, p.286.

of this was that the copper coins tended to accumulate in the hands of the shopkeepers and brewers of the major towns and cities, particularly London,[2] while the rest of the country was desperately short of coins. Contemporaries were fully aware that this was a virtual invitation to counterfeiters to step into the breach, and they rose to the occasion with gusto **(Fig 3b)**.[3]

Counterfeit copper coins (usually halfpennies, which were much commoner than farthings and much more important for day-to-day purchases) had been a growing problem since the late 1720s.[4] Until the middle of the century counterfeits were usually cast in moulds, but from then on they were frequently struck in screw presses.[5] A letter from E.Z. of Birmingham, published in the November 1752 *Gentleman's Magazine*, notes the change as happening very recently and warns that counterfeiters will in future be able to turn out very large numbers of more-convincing coins using this technology. An editorial note following E.Z.'s letter records that the tradesmen in Abingdon had recently held a meeting where they had resolved to accept no more 'Birmingham halfpence'. This is one of the first uses of this term, which was to make Birmingham notorious for the rest of the century.[6]

Unfortunately for Birmingham's reputation, while not every counterfeit halfpenny was made in Birmingham,[7] the town was certainly the major centre for the manufacture

Fig 3b. Obverse (top) and reverse (bottom), good quality copper counterfeit half-penny, dated '1774' (BMAG 1971 N 461).

---

2   Because the Royal Mint would not redeem (take back) its copper coins, banks would not deal with them, and they could not be used to pay bills or taxes (since they were not legal tender in amounts larger than a few pence). Businessmen might easily find themselves stuck with large amounts of halfpennies that they simply could not get rid of (Selgin, *Good Money*, p.22, p.282).

3   '... an insuperable difficulty has always been ... in getting them [i.e. copper coins] into circulation in all parts of the kingdom. Those who live at a distance will not send for them, and it is probably to this circumstance that the counterfeits have been made use of in preference to those hitherto coined at the Tower.' Privy Council report of 1799 quoted in P. Matthias, *English Trade Tokens. The Industrial Revolution Illustrated*, London, 1962, p.13.

4   Craig, *The Mint*, p.253. For a useful discussion of the earlier eighteenth-century counterfeits, see P.H. Robinson, 'The Dunchurch and Stafford finds of eighteenth-century halfpence and counterfeits', *British Numismatic Journal*, 41, 1972, pp.147-58, especially pp.156-8.

5   Selgin, *Good Money*, p.31.

6   The term also appears as 'Brummagem halfpence', using the town's nickname.

7   Counterfeits were also made in places like London, Sheffield, Dublin and even the North American colonies. J. Powell, *The Birmingham Coiners 1780-1816* unpublished MA dissertation, University of Sussex, 1977, p.45; Selgin, *Good Money*, p.29.

of counterfeit coin at this time. Indeed Birmingham might almost have been predestined for the role, since its metalworking industry was dominated by large numbers of small-scale workshops, where a few people might put to more nefarious use the skills and the machinery acquired for making buttons and other small die-stamped metal items.[8]

At its simplest a counterfeiting operation might comprise little more than a small gang which included someone with knowledge of the basic techniques, a safe place to make the counterfeits, and the ability to get rid of their products quickly.[9] Even operating at that scale the output might be substantial. Patrick Colquhoun, a London magistrate, estimated that two or three people could turn out 96,000 to 144,000 counterfeit halfpennies, representing £200-£300 face value, in a six-day week.[10] However, in Birmingham counterfeiting was often practised as a more open business and on a much larger scale, there being a ready market for its products, with makers selling to wholesale dealers who then sold on the products to the end users.[11] Boulton himself commented in a letter how some Birmingham makers had 'the audacity to hang up Signs in the street ALL SORTS OF COPPER COINS MADE HERE'.[12]

The law made things considerably easier for the counterfeiter than it might have done. Legally, while counterfeiting gold and silver coins was classed as high treason and punishable by death,[13] counterfeiting copper coins was classed as a misdemeanour and subject to very light penalties until an act of 1742 raised the penalty to two years imprisonment.[14] Even then the possession and transport of

---

8   Powell, *The Birmingham Coiners*, p.2; Selgin, *Good Money*, p.30. One commentator, in 1791, connected the manufacture of counterfeit halfpennies with 'shabby dishonest button makers in the dark lanes of Birmingham'. Powell, *The Birmingham Coiners*, p.5.

9   Powell, *The Birmingham Coiners*, p.46, p.48, p.66.

10   Figures cited in Selgin, *Good Money*, p.31.

11   Powell, *The Birmingham Coiners*, p.59; Selgin, *Good Money*, pp.29-30.

12   Letter, Matthew Boulton to Sir George Shuckburgh-Evelyn M.P., 9 March 1792 (MBP, MS 3782/12/37/50), cited in Selgin, *Good Money*, p.30. *Nota*: MBP is the abbreviation for Matthew Boulton Papers, Archives of Soho, Birmingham Central Library.

13   For men found guilty of counterfeiting gold or silver coins (and so of high treason) the full penalty was hanging, drawing and quartering, which was usually remitted to hanging by the eighteenth century. Since the full form of this punishment involved public nudity, it was not considered appropriate for women, who were instead burned at the stake. By the eighteenth century this had also been ameliorated and the victim was normally first strangled at the stake and the body then burned. Incredibly the last woman burned at the stake for counterfeiting was Catherine Murphy, who was executed at Newgate Gaol as late as March 1789. The law was changed in the following year and henceforth both men and women were simply hanged (*http://www.capitalpunishmentuk.org/burning.html*).

14   15 Geo. II c.28. R. Ruding, *Annals of the Coinage of Great Britain and its Dependencies*, volume 2 (3rd ed.), London, 1840, p.7. Those involved used to refer to the counterfeiting of gold or silver coins as a 'spiritual business' (since it was potentially fatal), whereas coining in copper was a 'temporal business' (leaving them only liable to time in prison). Powell, *The Birmingham Coiners*, p.50.

counterfeit coppers still remained legal.[15] Only in 1771 was the counterfeiting of copper coin finally raised to the status of a felony and the punishment increased again.[16]

The Royal Mint also did little to make life difficult for the counterfeiter.[17] Given the minting technology in general use at the time, the best defence against counterfeiting was to strike coins to a high weight so that their intrinsic value was reasonably close to their face value, to produce them from well-engraved dies that were hard to copy well, to mark their edges in some way so that cast copies became much harder to make, and to reproduce the dies mechanically so that each die (and hence each coin) was identical. Unfortunately the Royal Mint did none of these things. Changes in the price of copper meant that for much of the eighteenth century the face value of a halfpenny was roughly twice its intrinsic value (effectively, there was a farthing's worth of copper in a halfpenny),[18] giving counterfeiters an immediate profit even if they made their coins of unadulterated copper and of good weight (which most of them did not). In addition, the quality of Mint die engraving was not particularly high and there was enough variation in detail between individual dies to allow for

Fig 3c. Obverse (top) and reverse (bottom), heavily worn copper halfpenny of George II, date not visible (BMAG 2008.1413).

some uncertainty where genuine coins ended and good-quality counterfeits began.[19] Further, because the Royal Mint did not redeem its copper coins, they remained in circulation, becoming more and more worn until they were often reduced to little more than blank discs of copper **(Fig 3c)**.[20] This simplified the counterfeiter's task still

---

15 Craig, *The Mint*, p.252. In 1803 a new law made the possession of six counterfeit coppers an offence punishable by a substantial fine. Selgin, *Good Money*, p.295.

16 11 Geo. III c.40. Ruding, *Annals of the Coinage*, p.83; Craig, *The Mint*, p.252.

17 In truth the Royal Mint did not really seem to care very much about its copper coins, in contrast to the gold and silver that it saw as its real purpose. In 1757 Joseph Harris, the Mint's Assay Master, could say that 'Copper coins with us are properly not money, but a kind of token ... and useful in small home traffic' (Matthias, *English Trade Tokens*, p.14).

18 Selgin, *Good Money*, p.20.

19 Dyer/Gaspar, *Reform*, p.409, p.430; Selgin, *Good Money*, pp.280-84. As Selgin (p.33) points out, 'so far as the Mint was concerned, making [copper] coins was strictly a matter of putting legally authorised amounts of metal in them'.

20 The massive growth in the number of counterfeits made it harder for the Mint even to consider redeeming its copper coins. With so many good counterfeits in circulation there was a danger that the Mint would find itself buying back very large numbers of coins it had not made (Selgin, *Good Money*, p.33).

further since even an unskilled engraver could cut a die that carried only the vaguest outlines of the original design, resulting in counterfeits that would be virtually impossible to distinguish from a genuine worn regal coin.[21]

> The counterfeiter has only to procure a die (the sinking of which is within the ability of any workman in steel), with a faint outline of part of a bust upon it, and with a reverse totally plain: With this mean instrument he may secure a profit ...[22]

Others carried this even further and simply put blank discs into circulation.

Over time the quality of many counterfeits declined drastically **(Fig 3d)**. As competition between their makers intensified, the weights of the counterfeits were reduced[23] and they were made from progressively cheaper mixes of metal (with little copper in them), so that they were cheaper to produce and could be offered to customers at steadily reduced prices. In 1750 it was possible to buy thirty counterfeit halfpennies (=15d.) for a shilling (=12d.), but by 1770 you could buy thirty-six (=18d.) for the same amount.[24]

Fig 3d. Obverse (top) and reverse (bottom), poor quality copper counterfeit halfpenny, dated '1775' (BMAG 1932 N 107.13).

To be convicted of counterfeiting one had to produce products that were exact copies of the regal coins. The more cautious counterfeiters therefore changed the lettering or some other aspect of the design of their coins and so evaded a charge of counterfeiting by claiming that they were making medals or tokens. These 'evasive halfpennies' **(Fig 3e)** became much more common after the penalties for counterfeiting were raised in 1771, and their manufacture virtually a semi-respectable trade.[25]

This mixture of good and bad counterfeits, worn regal coins, blanks and evasives came to dominate the copper circulation pool. As early as 1753, Snelling estimated that

---

21   Selgin, *Good Money*, p.31, pp.286-8.

22   Rev. Rogers Ruding, 1797, quoted in Selgin, *Good Money*, p.287. The reference is to dies for counterfeit silver coins, but is equally applicable to the copper coinage.

23   The Royal Mint struck 46 halfpennies from a pound of copper; counterfeiters might produce 72. Selgin, *Good Money*, p.31.

24   Craig, *The Mint*, p.253.

25   Powell, *The Birmingham Coiners*, p.14; Craig, *The Mint*, pp.252-3; Selgin, *Good Money*, pp.32-3. 'Evasives' is the term in common use today; Craig memorably described them as 'semi-halfpence'.

40-50% of the copper coin in circulation was counterfeit.[26] Estimates for later in the century vary, but they are all higher. In the 1770s Boulton thought that two-thirds were counterfeit or otherwise unofficial; a 1787 Royal Mint study of a sample of halfpennies concluded that only 8% were genuine; while Pinkerton in 1789 estimated that 98% were counterfeit.[27]

From 1787 another unofficial element was added to this already eclectic mix with the appearance of trade tokens (usually copper halfpennies). The first of these was issued by Thomas Williams, the Copper King, who ran the Parys Mines Company of Anglesey. The idea soon caught on and tokens were issued by a large number of other issuers, generally merchants or businesses based in the town or county named on the tokens. These tokens relied on public trust in the issuer's promise to redeem his tokens on demand for coin of the realm, so many of them had only a very local circulation. However, those issued by Williams and a number of other major players were widely trusted and enjoyed a virtually nationwide circulation. Like the counterfeits, most trade tokens were struck in Birmingham (some indeed by Boulton himself).[28] In essence, token issuers, like counterfeiters, were putting their own coins into circulation to meet a very obvious need, but the big difference was that token issuers (at least the respectable ones) promised to redeem their products.[29] Things began to break down when some tokens themselves began to be counterfeited and others were put into circulation with no intent to redeem them.[30]

Fig 3e. Obverse (top) and reverse (bottom), copper 'evasive' halfpenny, SHAKESPEARE / RULE BRITANNIA, '1771' (BMAG 1964 N 2139) (Reproduced courtesy of Birmingham Museum and Art Gallery).

It can be argued that this explosion of counterfeits and similar unofficial pieces was economically beneficial, and that these pieces were accepted in circulation

---

26 T. Snelling, *View of the Copper Coinage of England*, London, 1766, p.44.

27 Doty, *The Soho Mint*, p.15; Craig, *The Mint*, p.253; Robinson, 'The Dunchurch and Stafford finds ...', p.156; Selgin, *Good Money*, p.29. Selgin quotes a 1789 Royal Mint estimate that there were 1,200 tons of regal halfpennies in circulation as against about 3,000 tons of counterfeits. Selgin, *Good Money*, p.287 n.21.

28 Craig, *The Mint*, p.254; Powell, *The Birmingham Coiners*, pp.16-17.

29 Powell, *The Birmingham Coiners*, p.66.

30 See below for an approach made to Matthew Boulton to produce counterfeit tokens. However, tokens were never counterfeited on anything like the same scale as the regal halfpennies. It was mainly those with a wide circulation that were so targeted.

because they were quite simply all that was available to fill the gap left by the lack of coins from the Royal Mint. People used them *faut de mieux*.[31] This must be particularly true of the really poor quality counterfeits that could never have fooled anyone into believing they were genuine coins.[32] The Royal Mint might complain that 'the Public suffer themselves to be imposed on by the most bungling imitations',[33] but in truth the public had no other choice. Many employers certainly found it useful to be able to buy locally the small change that they needed to help pay their workers. If they could buy the coins at a discount, then so much the better.[34]

However, not everyone was happy with the situation. Complaints about the condition of the copper coinage were heard from the earliest days of George III and they grew steadily in volume.[35] Shopkeepers, innkeepers and other traders, who had to accept irregular coins from working people or see them take their custom elsewhere, could find themselves seriously out of pocket.[36] Meetings were held around the country to complain about the number of counterfeits and to try and prevent their circulation. We have seen above how such a meeting was held as early as 1752 in Abingdon. In February 1783 a meeting of the inhabitants of Westminster resulted in a petition against the circulation of counterfeit halfpence which was presented to the House of Commons.[37] The traders of Birmingham itself were just as hostile to the counterfeiters and their products. In February 1776 a meeting of the 'principal inhabitants' of the town was held which decided to offer a reward of £20 for information. Two years later, in 1778, the 'principal traders' met at a coffee house in Cherry Street and signed an agreement to prosecute offenders. In 1780, the town officers announced that they were determined to put an end to the manufacture of base coin once and for all.[38] However, it was the workers who suffered most through being compelled to accept bad coin in their pay, which might be refused in the local shops, or only accepted at a discount.[39] As

---

31   Craig, *The Mint*, p.253: as Craig says, 'Ordinary folk, if short of small change, cared nothing about either intrinsic value, high quality of copper, pattern or limits of legal tender.' Visitors to Italy in the 1970s, when there was a similar shortage of small change, found themselves being given telephone tokens, ballpoint pens and even sweets in place of the unavailable low-value coins.

32   Selgin, *Good Money*, p.32.

33   Quoted in Dyer/Gaspar, *Reform*, p.436.

34   Powell, *The Birmingham Coiners*, p.8. As we have seen, in 1770 an employer could buy 18 pence worth of counterfeit halfpennies for a shilling, meaning that for every £3 of wages he paid in counterfeits he made a saving of £1.

35   See, for example, Ruding, *Annals of the Coinage*, p.81 and p.83; Selgin, *Good Money*, p.32.

36   Powell, *The Birmingham Coiners*, p.15; Selgin, *Good Money*, p.33. See note 2, above.

37   Ruding, *The Annals of the Coinage*, p.92.

38   W.J. Davis, *The Token Coinage of Warwickshire*, Birmingham, 1895, p.xiii.

39   Powell, *The Birmingham Coiners*, p.15.

an unabashedly paternalistic employer, their plight appears to have been close to Boulton's heart.[40]

As a large-scale employer Boulton would have been fully aware of the difficulty of finding adequate coins to pay his workforce and he might have been expected to take advantage of the counterfeits so readily available just a mile or so from his manufactory in Soho. Instead he was quite consistent in his desire to see counterfeiting stopped and a reformed coinage introduced.[41] He gave a number of reasons why he was so determined. First he wanted to prevent workers from being defrauded by having to accept poor quality coins from their employers, and thus save the wider community from the effects these coins had when they entered circulation.

> The Publick has sustained and must inevitably sustain great loss by the illegal practice of counterfeiting halfpence, which has been lately carried to a greater height than was ever before known and seems still to increase insomuch that it is now too common a Custom among many of the lower class of Manufacturers and Traders to purchase these counterfeit halfpence at little more than half their nominal value and to pay, with this money, their workmen and Labourers greatly to the injury of the honest part of the community and to the detriment of Trade …[42]

On a more personal level Boulton had become fascinated with the technology of minting and had genuinely come to believe that he and his mint were the only means of solving the counterfeits problem. He also hoped that this would raise both his own and his home town's reputation.[43] In addition Boulton had strong business reasons for wanting the contract to strike a reformed copper coinage. In the 1780s his various businesses were effectively being kept afloat by the premiums being paid by the Cornish copper mines that had acquired Boulton and Watt steam engines.[44] Unfortunately, the Cornish copper industry was being challenged by cheaper copper from Anglesey. A major coinage contract that would require hundreds of tons of copper would be a very useful thing.[45]

---

40 Powell, *The Birmingham Coiners*, p.31.

41 Powell, *The Birmingham Coiners*, p.44.

42 From a paper prepared by Boulton in December 1789 for the Privy Council Committee on Coin (MBP, MS 3782/12/97/6) in response to a Royal Mint memorandum laying out the reasons why there was no need for a new copper coinage. Boulton's paper is misdated to 20 December 1787 by Powell in *The Birmingham Coiners*, p.14.

43 Doty, *The Soho Mint*, pp.15-16, pp.26-7; Powell, *The Birmingham Coiners*, p.44; Selgin, *Good Money*, pp.65-6.

44 Companies agreed to pay an annual premium equivalent to one-third of the fuel savings they made from using the new engine. Selgin, *Good Money*, pp.67-8.

45 Selgin, *Good Money*, pp.66-71.

Boulton took his first step towards becoming a major coin maker when he undertook to supply the East India Company with copper coins for Bencoolen (now Benkulen), one of its holdings on Sumatra. In a convoluted exercise, the Company supplied the copper to the Soho Manufactory, where the blanks were made. These were then shipped to London and struck into coins on manually-operated presses that Boulton had installed in a Company warehouse.[46] From this experience Boulton drew the lesson that it would be better to have his own mint at Soho, where he could control every part of the process, and that it should be equipped with steam-powered presses.[47] Borne along by his enthusiasm, and convinced a government contract for a new copper coinage would soon be his, between 1786 and 1789 Boulton invested several thousand pounds constructing the Soho Mint, the most modern in the world. Unfortunately, the government kept putting off a decision about a new coinage for the better part of a decade, a period when Boulton saw his hopes regularly raised and dashed and he was forced to take on all sorts of work to keep the mint alive.[48]

In his campaign for a reformed copper coinage during these years, Boulton made great claims for his mint and its products. He could point to the high quality of the tokens he produced – struck from skilfully engraved dies on perfectly round flans of regular thickness – which were much harder to counterfeit than the Royal Mint's halfpennies.[49] This was made very clear in 1788 when both Boulton and the Royal Mint supplied the Privy Council Committee on Coin with pattern halfpennies, struck from dies engraved by Jean-Pierre Droz and Lewis Pingo respectively **(Fig 4a, b)**.[50] Even a cursory glance reveals how much better the standard of die-cutting and striking was at Soho, and how much more regular its flan was.

---

46   Doty, *The Soho Mint*, pp.299-301; B.M. Gould, 'Matthew Boulton's East India Company mint in London, 1786-88', *Seaby Coin and Medal Bulletin*, no.612, August 1969, pp.270-7.

47   Selgin, *Good Money*, pp.63-4.

48   Doty, *The Soho Mint*, pp.50-51, pp.302-15; Selgin, *Good Money*, pp.114-19; see also D. Symons, '"Bringing to Perfection the Art of Coining": what did they make at the Soho Mint?' in S. Mason (ed.), *Matthew Boulton: Selling What All the World Desires*, New Haven and London, 2009, pp.89-98 and D. Symons, 'Matthew Boulton and the Royal Mint', in M. Dick (ed.), *Matthew Boulton: A Revolutionary Player*, Studley, 2009, pp.170-184.

49   Selgin, *Good Money*, p.285. Of course, if Boulton did not give token issuers high quality products they were free to take their custom to other makers. This was not a problem the Royal Mint faced – at least not yet.

50   Droz was a Swiss die-engraver lured over to Soho by Boulton at great expense. Unfortunately, Boulton was never able to get much work out of him and their relationship soon broke down. For the full story see J.G. Pollard, 'Matthew Boulton and J.-P. Droz', *Numismatic Chronicle*, 7th series, vol. 8, 1968, pp.241-65; Doty, *The Soho Mint*, pp.26-45. In a letter to his son of 30 July 1790, Boulton describes Droz as 'the most ungratefull, most ungenerous, & basest man I ever had any concern with' (MBP, MS 3782/13/36/48).

However, in his enthusiasm (and determination to win the contract) Boulton was liable to push his claims too far.

> ... I have executed and perfected such an apparatus of Machinery as will make Coin not only superior in Beauty & Workmanship to that of any Nation in Europe but also so manufactured in consequence of the peculiar construction of my Machinery that Counterfeiting will be affectually prevented and consequently the number of Capital Offences diminished.[51]

In fact, it was not his steam presses that made his products harder to counterfeit, but the quality of his flan preparation, his die engraving, and the use of a collar in striking that did this. Droz's pattern halfpenny was struck on a manually-operated press. What steam technology would do in due course was to give Boulton the ability to make lots of coins faster and more regularly than before.[52] Contemporaries were clearly dazzled by the steam-powered machinery, something that only Boulton and the Soho Mint could boast.[53] In fact, they were so impressed that when the

Fig 4a. Obverse (top) and reverse (bottom), copper pattern halfpenny of the Soho Mint, engraved by J.-P. Droz, 1788 (BMAG 1969 N 637).

need for a new copper coinage suddenly became urgent the Royal Mint was ignored and it was to Matthew Boulton that the government turned.

It was a financial crisis in February 1797 that gave Boulton his great opportunity.[54] The costs of the war with France were draining the Bank of England's gold reserves so fast that on 26 February the Privy Council was forced to tell the Bank to stop redeeming its banknotes for gold.[55] To prevent a collapse of confidence in the financial system, the government took a number of measures to address the problem

---

51 From the paper prepared by Matthew Boulton for the Privy Council Committee on Coin, December 1789 (MBP, MS 3782/12/97/6).

52 Doty, *The Soho Mint*, p.15; Powell, *The Birmingham Coiners*, p.27; Selgin, *Good Money*, pp.290-1, p.297.

53 Selgin, *Good Money*, p.284.

54 For the events described here, see G.P. Dyer, 'The currency crisis of 1797', *British Numismatic Journal*, 72, 2002, pp.135-42.

55 For the background to this crisis see Selgin, *Good Money*, pp.155-6.

over the next few days. The Bank of England and the 'country' banks in England and Wales were authorised to issue banknotes of less than £5 in value, which had formerly been banned. The government also decided, as an emergency measure, to countermark the Bank's large stock of Spanish silver dollars and put them into circulation as silver tokens with a face value of 4s. 9d. The experiment was not a success,[56] but we will return to these dollars later.

The new banknotes and the countermarked dollars were intended to relieve problems caused by a shortage of gold coins in circulation. To overcome the shortage of low-value silver coins a new copper coinage was also decided on. Copper pennies and twopences were issued for the first time, rather than the traditional farthings and halfpennies.[57] Accordingly, on 3 March 1797 Lord Liverpool wrote to Boulton on behalf of the Privy Council Committee on Coin, inviting him to London to discuss the new coinage.

> There is no Man who can better judge of the Propriety of the Measure, and of the Plan that ought to be adopted, in issuing a Coinage of this Nature, than yourself: and no one will execute it with more Accuracy and Expedition.[58]

Fig 4b. Obverse (top) and reverse (bottom), copper pattern halfpenny of the Royal Mint, engraved by Lewis Pingo, 1788 (BMAG 1969 N 623) (Reproduced courtesy of Birmingham Museum and Art Gallery).

A delighted Boulton left for London immediately and attended a meeting of the Committee on the 7 March. Although they received two rival offers, the Committee's report, submitted on 28 March 1797, recommended that the contract should be awarded to Boulton.[59] Tellingly, the Royal Mint seems never to have been seriously

---

56   H.E. Manville, *Tokens of the Industrial Revolution. Foreign Silver Coins Countermarked for Use in Great Britain, c.1787-1828*, London, 2001, pp.3-4.

57   Pennies and twopences could replace low value silver coins in a way that halfpennies and farthings could not. The government was also afraid that a new issue of halfpennies might simply drive the counterfeits *et al.* out of circulation before enough new coins were available to replace them. Dyer, 'The currency crisis', p.140; Craig, *The Mint*, pp.264-5; Dyer/Gaspar, *Reform*, p.446.

58   Letter, Lord Liverpool to Matthew Boulton, 3 March 1797 (MBP, MS 3782/12/General correspondence 1797/35). Selgin gives the full text of the letter. Selgin, *Good Money*, pp.162-3.

59   Selgin, *Good Money*, p.163.

considered for this work. The result was the famous Cartwheel coins. The name comes from the raised rim which surrounded the design on each side of the coin and which reminded contemporaries of the iron-shod wheels on carts. Using steam presses to strike very large numbers of such large coins forced Boulton to use dies cut in low relief, since it made it impossible to give each coin the several blows necessary to produce higher relief designs. Boulton added the raised rims to help protect the shallow designs from excessive wear while the coins were in circulation.[60]

Royal assent for the new coinage was given on 9 June 1797,[61] and Soho Mint swung into action producing the coins. The Royal Proclamation making them legal tender, issued on 26 July 1797, was noted in the *Aris's Birmingham Gazette* of 31 July.

> A Proclamation has been issued by his Majesty (our readers will see) for giving legal currency to Mr. BOULTON'S COINAGE; and his beautiful pennies will very soon be in circulation. The mint at Soho has been for some time at work, and the business is prosecuted with so much assiduity, that twenty tons of copper (making *seven hundred and sixteen thousand eight hundred* pennies) are *weekly* struck in the different dies.[62]

Boulton may have confidently declared his new coins could only be struck on his new presses and would be more difficult to forge than any others, but he soon found that he had seriously underestimated the ingenuity of his fellow citizens.[63] Undeterred by a new act, signed into law on 19 July, which increased the penalties for counterfeiting the new coinage,[64] the Birmingham coiners were turning out counterfeits within just a few weeks, as *Aris's Birmingham Gazette* again makes clear.

> Such is the astonishing *perfection* to which the art of villainy is now arrived, that Mr. Boulton's new copper coinage has already been counterfeited with surprising neatness and accuracy. The counterfeits are composed of two thin sheets of copper, between which is placed a piece of lead. They are considerably lighter than the genuine coin, and, when struck with a key or a knife, produce a dull leaden sound – a precaution to which the public will do well to attend. *See Mr. Boulton's advertisement.*[65]

---

60 Selgin, *Good Money*, p.292.
61 Dyer/Gaspar, *Reform*, pp.446-7; Doty, *The Soho Mint*, p.315.
62 *Aris's Birmingham Gazette*, Monday, 31 July 1797, Vol. LVI, no.2907, p.3. The text of the royal proclamation appears at the top left-hand corner of the same page; an image of the proclamation can be found in Doty, *The Soho Mint*, p.316.
63 Powell, *The Birmingham Coiners*, p.33; Selgin, *Good Money*, p.174, p.177, p.292.
64 Selgin, *Good Money*, p.174. The act is 37 Geo. III c.126. Ruding, *Annals of the Coinage*, pp.94-5).
65 *Aris's Birmingham Gazette*, Monday, 4 September 1797 (Vol. LVI, no.2912), p.3.

The advertisement referred to appeared on the same page and makes it quite clear how stung Boulton was by this development and how determined he was to try and put an end to it.

NEW COPPER COIN

Information having been received, that the COPPER COIN legalized by Act of Parliament and his Majesty's Proclamation, which is issued from SOHO MINT, has been COUNTERFEITED – I hereby offer a Reward of ONE HUNDRED GUINEAS, over and above the Sum allowed by Government, upon Conviction of any Person or Persons, who shall have been concerned in making or issuing such Counterfeits.

MATTHEW BOULTON.

Soho, September 2, 1797.[66]

Boulton placed a second notice, dated 6 October, in *Pierson's Paper* offering a 'handsome reward' for information on those who were guilty of counterfeiting the new coinage. As the description given there makes clear, it was cast copies that were the immediate problem.[67] These cast copies took advantage of the almost incredible fact that, when designing the cartwheels, Boulton had apparently fallen for his own propaganda and had ignored one of the major anti-counterfeiting devices that we have already mentioned – he made them with a plain edge instead of using some kind of edge marking, which would have made the counterfeiter's life much harder.[68]

Despite Boulton's best efforts, counterfeit cartwheel pennies continued to appear. Some were much more sophisticated than the initial relatively crude cast or plated copies and took advantage of another design feature of the cartwheels – the shallow designs that the use of steam presses had dictated. It proved much easier than Boulton had anticipated for the more skilled counterfeiters to engrave dies which copied these designs quite closely.[69]

In January 1799 Boulton received a letter from an informant signing himself W.P., who offered information about where counterfeits were being produced in Birmingham.[70] In fact W.P. told him of no less than three workshops producing counterfeit cartwheels. Armed with this information Boulton arranged with one of

66 *Aris's Birmingham Gazette*, Monday, 4 September 1797 (Vol. LVI, no.2912), p.3.
67 Selgin, *Good Money*, pp.174-5.
68 Selgin, *Good Money*, pp.281-2, p.295.
69 Selgin, *Good Money*, p.295.
70 The full text of the letter can be found in Selgin, *Good Money*, p.175.

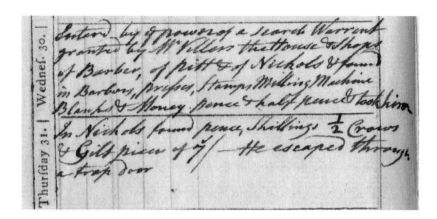

Fig 5. Entry in Matthew Boulton's diary *for Wednesday 30 January 1799 (MBP, MS 3782/12/107/27) (Reproduced courtesy of Birmingham Archives and Heritage).*

the town magistrates that he and fourteen of his workers would go with the town constables and carry out simultaneous raids on the suspect premises on 30 January.[71] He recorded the outcome in his diary **(Fig 5)**.

> Enterd by ye power of a search Warrant granted by Mr. Villers the House & Shops of Barber, of Pitt & of Nichols & found in Barbers, presses, Stamps Milling Machine Blanks & Money pence and halfpence & took him. In Nichols found pence, shillings, ½ crowns & Gilt pieces of 7/- He escaped through a trap door.[72]

The third man accused, Pitt, an 'old offender', was also apprehended, but seems to have escaped prosecution.[73]

The case against Richard Barber appeared to be open-and-shut since he had been caught red-handed, and his trial was set for the Warwick Assize in March 1799. To establish the case in law, however, Boulton needed an official from the Royal Mint to attend the trial and confirm that the coins seized were indeed counterfeit so, on 13 February, he wrote to John Vernon, the Mint's solicitor,

---

71 Selgin, *Good Money*, p.176. Boulton paid W.P. £50 for his information. Powell, *The Birmingham Coiners*, p.48.

72 Matthew Boulton's diary for 1799 (MBP, MS 3782/12/107/27), entry for Wednesday 30 January. It is worth pointing out that Boulton had celebrated his 70th birthday in the previous September. Despite his age, he would not have wanted to miss out on such excitement. Nichols's escape was more dramatic than Boulton's brief account suggests – see Selgin, *Good Money*, p.176.

73 Selgin, *Good Money*, p.176.

asking him to send someone to give the required evidence.[74] At this point, it seems that Boulton may have fallen foul of the ill-feeling harboured for him by the Mint establishment, for it was a month before Vernon replied, saying that he would be sending his assistant, Mr Powell, accompanied by one of the Mint's moneyers. Unfortunately for Boulton, Powell did not reach Warwick until 26 March, a day after the judge had been compelled to dismiss the case against Barber for lack of evidence and free him, commenting as he did so that 'the dilatory proceedings of the Mint were very shameful but by no means unusual'.[75]

Boulton himself was in London when the trial collapsed, but one of his employees, William Cheshire, wrote to give him the news.

> … I have now to inform you that the witnesses against Barber were released from their recognizances before I left Warwick. And all the Prisoners committed for Coining were yesterday discharged by Proclamation.[76]

Vernon made a sort of apology to Boulton for Powell's delay, but, to add insult to injury, he also suggested that Boulton might himself be guilty of counterfeiting since he had minted more coins than his original contract allowed for before a second order had actually been signed, meaning he had technically been striking royal coins without legal authority to do so. Cheshire certainly suspected that the Royal Mint had deliberately ruined the prosecution and saw this as further evidence that 'the Mint are endeavouring … to give a death blow to your coinage'.[77] To add to Boulton's frustration he discovered that his informant, W.P., William Phillips, had also been guilty of counterfeiting cartwheels and had informed on the others for private reasons.[78]

Remarkably, one of Barber's counterfeit cartwheels has survived and is now preserved in the collections of Birmingham Museum and Art Gallery **(Fig 6a)**.[79] It is an excellent piece of workmanship, produced from skilfully-engraved dies, and only

74 Letter, Matthew Boulton to John Vernon, 13 February 1799 (cited by Powell, *The Birmingham Coiners*, p.33).
75 For this episode see Selgin, *Good Money*, pp.176-7; Powell, *The Birmingham Coiners*, pp.33-4. For Boulton's relationship with the Mint, see Symons, 'Matthew Boulton and the Royal Mint'.
76 Copy letter, William Cheshire to Matthew Boulton, 26 March 1799 (MBP, MS 3782/3/227).
77 Selgin, *Good Money*, p.177; Powell, *The Birmingham Coiners*, pp.33-4; letter, William Cheshire to Matthew Boulton, 26 March 1799 (cited by Powell, *The Birmingham Coiners*, p.34).
78 He may well be the same man as the William Phillips who was himself charged at Warwick Assize in 1807 for counterfeiting Prussian coins. Selgin, p.176; Powell, *The Birmingham Coiners*, pp.57-8.
79 Accession no. 1976 N 25. It was presented to the museum in 1976 as part of a group of miscellaneous Soho pieces by a descendant of John Phillp, a Boulton protégé and Soho designer and engraver.

let down by its slightly low weight and by the fact that the rim is less well-defined than on genuine coins. It was struck on a manually-operated screw press, which rather made a nonsense of all Boulton's claims for the unique and un-counterfeitable nature of pieces struck on his steam presses, and probably explains why he was so outraged by such counterfeits.[80] It is in a paper wrapper **(Fig 6b)** which is inscribed

> 1797 / Counterfeit Penny / made by – Barber of / Birmingham who was com / mitted to Warwick & would / have been convicted but for / the delay of M[r]. Powell the / Solicitor to the Mint. / from W. Coley.

Boulton struck further issues of regal copper coins dated 1799 and 1806-7. For these he abandoned the cartwheel's distinctive raised rim and incuse lettering, which had so obviously failed to prevent them being counterfeited. Instead he added diagonal milled lines to the edges of the coins, which would make casting copies much harder. He also struck these issues on slightly concave flans, which would present the counterfeiter with another problem to overcome.[81] Although some counterfeits are known of these issues, the problem was much reduced. However, the old halfpennies and farthings issued prior to 1775 (together with the mass of counterfeits, blank flans and evasives) had not been withdrawn when the Soho coins were put into circulation, so it was still open to the counterfeiters to carry on producing copies of the old worn coins as they had long been doing.[82] Even as late as March 1807 the

Fig 6a. Obverse (top) and reverse (bottom), counterfeit copper cartwheel penny made in Birmingham by Richard Barber, with (Fig 6b. below) an original paper wrapper (BMAG 1976 N 25) (Reproduced courtesy of Birmingham Museum and Art Gallery).

---

80   Selgin, *Good Money*, p.177.

81   Doty, *The Soho Mint*,p.320; Dyer/Gaspar, *Reform*, p.448.

82   Craig, *The Mint*, pp.266-7. The government was put off withdrawing the old coins by the sheer expense involved, especially while the country was at war with the French.

Privy Council Committee on Coin was forced to admit that 'counterfeit halfpence are now nearly as abundant in … London as they have been at any former time'. The situation was not rectified until the Royal Mint finally withdrew much of the old copper from circulation in 1814-17.[83]

Boulton was involved in one more national issue where problems posed by counterfeiters played a significant part. As we have seen, in 1797 the government authorised the Bank of England to countermark a large number of Spanish 'dollars'[84] and put them into circulation as silver tokens with a face value of 4s. 9d.[85] The countermark chosen was a small head of George III, which was struck onto the head of the Spanish king, giving rise to a number of satirical squibs, including the well-known

> The Bank to make their Spanish dollars pass,
> Stamped the head of a fool on the head of an ass.

Unfortunately for Bank and government, the face value of the countermarked tokens was slightly higher than the price at which unstamped dollars could be bought on the bullion market, which made it profitable to buy up coins and apply fake countermarks to them. The more unscrupulous simply applied fake countermarks to counterfeit coins. The Bank was soon forced to announce the recall of its tokens and the dollars were reduced to the status of bullion silver once more.[86]

In 1804 the government decided to try the same thing again, but once more it rapidly became clear that such countermarked tokens were simply too easy to counterfeit.[87] However, Boulton had been experimenting and proposed a radical solution to the directors of the Bank: instead of countermarking the dollars, he would use the power of his steam presses to overstrike them with new designs, obliterating the old designs in the process.[88] The Bank agreed to his proposal and in 1804 Soho produced just over a million of what Boulton always referred as 'regenerated dollars' **(Fig 7)**.[89] In fact some elements of the original design often remained just visible, but typically Boulton turned this into a positive by arguing that

---

83 For this paragraph in general, see Selgin, *Good Money*, p.288.
84 As the British called them; they were actually Spanish coins of eight reales.
85 Dyer, 'The *currency* crisis of 1797'; Dyer/Gaspar, *Reform*, p.449. See also n.56 above.
86 Manville, *Tokens*, p.4; Craig, *The Mint*, p.261; Selgin, *Good Money*, pp.159-60.
87 Craig, *The Mint*, p.262.
88 For what follows see Doty, *The Soho Mint*, pp.326-7.
89 Selgin, *Good Money*, pp.198-9; Doty, *The Soho Mint* p.327. Another 3.5 million dollars were overstruck in 1809-11, although they all bore the date 1804.

having to reproduce such traces would make the counterfeiter's task still more difficult.[90] Once again, however, he had underestimated the ingenuity of the counterfeiters and high quality copies were arriving at the Bank of England within a matter of days.[91]

Given his antipathy to counterfeiters, it is ironic that Boulton himself should have been approached on a number of occasions to produce copies of various coins and tokens. For example, on 1 November 1794, Andrew Collins, his agent in Copenhagen, wrote to him as follows:

> I have got here acquainted with M^r. Constantine Brun, a Merchant of respectability, who informs me that some time ago he wrote to you concerning some Portuguese Coins wishing to be inform'd whether you would undertake to make for him gold Johannes's, (I believe they are generally called Joes) whole as well as half Pieces: the whole ones to weigh 7½dwt Penny Weight and he requested your Advice at what rate you would deliver them in London.
>
> Mr Brun has receiv'd no Answer to his Letter, and being in Company with me at a Gent^s. House, & understanding that I am your Agent: he desired me to write to you Sir, on the Subject. I will not pretend to give an Opinion

Fig 7. Obverse (top) and reverse (bottom), Bank of England silver dollar token, overstruck on a Spanish 8 reales piece (BMAG 1932 N 285 434) (Reproduced courtesy of Birmingham Museum and Art Gallery).

as to the propriety or Impropriety of such an Undertaking: you are certainly best Judge of it. But in either case you will be pleased to give him a Line in answer to his Question, whether or not you can supply him? He talks of wanting from £5 to £10,000 Sterl^g worth pr Annum .... from inquiries I have made here, I learn that he is a Gentleman of Property – a Merchant who trades

---

90   Dyer/Gaspar, *Reform*, p.453.

91   Selgin, *Good Money*, p.295; Ruding, *Annals of the Coinage*, p.102. Counterfeiting of Bank dollars was not a crime as they were legally not regal coins but tokens. Prosecution was a civil matter for the Bank of England to pursue. Powell, *The Birmingham Coiners*, p.50.

chiefly to the West Indies (where, apparently he wishes to diffuse these Joe's; as they are almost the only Currency there) he is known here for a Man of Probity and Character.[92]

Brun's original letter does not seem to survive, nor is there any sign of a reply from Boulton to Collins, but unsurprisingly there is no evidence that Soho ever struck such illicit coins.

The coins that Brun wanted copied were the Portuguese gold half dobra of 6,400 reis (and its half). These coins were originally struck in 1722 by John V (1706-50), hence the name 'Johannes', from the Latin form of the king's name which appeared on the coins. In Britain and its American and West Indian colonies these coins were popularly known as 'Joes', a nickname that remained appropriate when John V was succeeded by Joseph I (1750-77). Thanks to the discovery of large deposits of gold at Minas Gerais in Brazil, Portuguese gold coins were struck in very large quantities in the eighteenth century. They formed an important part of the gold circulating in Britain, and came to dominate the gold currency pool in the Caribbean. Although Boulton did not get involved, others were less scrupulous, and lightweight and debased forgeries were struck in Europe and shipped to the West Indies by merchants like Brun.[93] Eventually, they became such a nuisance that drastic steps were taken – legislation on St Vincent in 1798 regulated what coins could be used on the island, established minimum weights for these coins, and decreed the death penalty for those found guilty of importing or issuing base or lightweight coin in the future. Interestingly, the weight specified for a 'single Joe' was 7½ pennyweights (dwt), exactly the standard that Brun had specified for his copies. This was only about 80% of the official weight of a genuine coin (9 dwt 5 grains).[94]

Had Boulton carried out this work he would certainly have been breaking the law. Since 1572 it had been illegal to counterfeit foreign gold or silver coins that were not current legal tender within England.[95] In 1797 new legislation made the counterfeiting or passing of foreign gold or silver coins into a felony, for which the

---

92 Letter, Andrew Collins (Copenhagen) to Matthew Boulton, 1 November 1794 (MBP, MS 3782/12/ 39/298).

93 F. Pridmore, *The Coins of the British Commonwealth of Nations to the end of the Reign of George VI, 1952. Part 3, Bermuda, British Guiana, British Honduras and the British West Indies*, London, 1965, pp.8-9, and then *passim* for references to lightweight Joes on various islands.

94 Pridmore, *The Coins of the British Commonwealth of Nations*, pp.319-21. For some further context on this episode, see D.Vice, 'A trial strike of a Birmingham counterfeiter's die', *Format* 37, 1988, p.8 (sales list produced by Format Coins, Birmingham).

95 Ruding, *Annals of the Coinage*, volume I, p.345. The statute is 14 Eliz. I c.3.

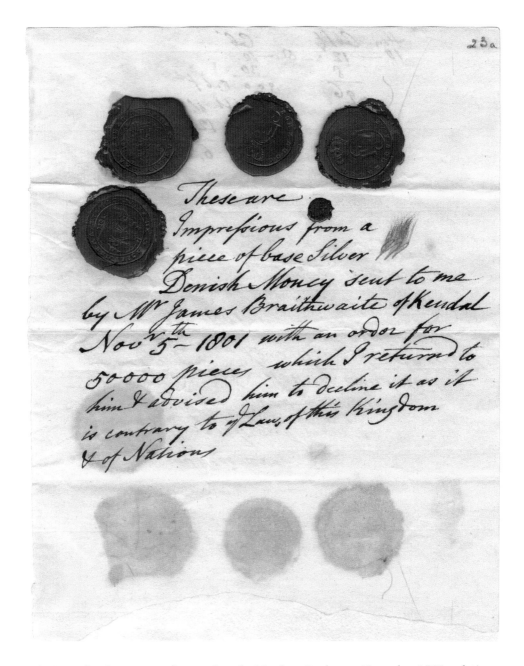

Fig 8. Undated memorandum *written by Matthew Boulton, c.November 1801, relating to a request that he make copies of Danish billon coins for the West Indies (MBP, MS 3782/12/46/352-23a) (Reproduced courtesy of Birmingham Archives and Heritage).*

penalty was transportation for seven years.[96] A few years later Boulton received a request that would have put him in breach of this new legislation. This time the approach was from a source nearer to home:

> Sir
> I have taken the liberty to Inclose you a Medal for w[h] I believe 50,000 will be wanted I will thank you first to say if it Conveniant to do them for us and then the price they will cost – I am S[r] for [illegible] & C[o]
> > y[r]. Most Ob[t] Serv[t]
> > James Braithwaite
>
> Kendal 5th Nov[r] 1801.[97]

Again there seems to be no trace of Boulton's letter replying to Braithwaite, but the tenor of that reply is made crystal clear by an undated memorandum in Boulton's own hand **(Fig 8)**. Attached to the top of the sheet are four wax impressions taken from the 'medal' that Braithwaite had sent as a sample (two impressions each of the obverse and reverse). These show that the 'medal' was a Danish billon (base silver) 12 skilling coin, struck in Copenhagen in 1767 for use in the Danish Virgin Islands. Boulton's text reads

> These are Impressions from a piece of base silver Danish Money sent to me by M[r] James Braithwaite of Kendal Nov[r] 5th 1801 with an order for 50000 pieces which I returned to him & advised him to decline it as it is contrary to y[e] Laws of this Kingdom & of Nations.[98]

The Danish Virgin Islands (St Thomas, St John and St Croix) were sold to the U.S.A. in 1916 and are today known as the United States Virgin Islands. In March 1801 they were occupied by Britain following Danish involvement in the Russian-inspired League of Armed Neutrality, which Britain saw as a pro-French movement. They were handed back to Danish control in March 1802. The request to Boulton for 50,000 counterfeits, made on 5 November 1801, falls squarely within this period of British occupation and gives every impression of having been made by a trading company intending (none too scrupulously) to exploit the commercial opportunities offered by this new situation. Given the

---

96   37 Geo. III c.126. Ruding, *Annals of the Coinage*, volume 1, pp.94-5.

97   Letter, James Braithwaite (Kendal) to Matthew Boulton, 5 November 1801 (MBP, MS 3782/12/46/352).

98   Undated memorandum by Matthew Boulton (MBP, MS 3782/12/46/352).

lack of detail in Braithwaite's letter, we cannot say for sure whether the coins ordered would have been lightweight copies, like those wanted by Brun, but this seems likely.

The third approach we will consider here arrived in 1796 from Dr J. Solomon of Liverpool, who did not want counterfeits of foreign coins, but rather copies of the Druid's head tokens produced by Thomas Williams's Parys Mines Company. Boulton himself had actually struck some 2,150,000 Parys halfpennies and 34,000 pennies for Williams over the period 1789-92. Solomon's initial enquiry was as follows.

> Sir
> I can take 1 Ton per week of the Anglesea penny pieces 18½ or 19 to the lb. Please to acquaint me with the lowest price for <u>ready</u> money –
> I am Sir, very respectfully
> Your Obed[t]. Serv[t].
> J. Solomon[99]

Boulton's reply, while clearly keen to pick up any business that might be available, was uncompromising.

> In reply to your fav[t] of y[e] 29 Ultim[o] I can undertake to make any quantity of Copper pieces you can dispose of, in any time you may want them in, & I can make them of a superior quality to the provincial tokens commonly made as mine will be perfectly round & with bright edges & struck in Collers but I cannot Strike any pieces wth the name of (& saying payable by) the Anglesey Co as that would be something like forging a note of Hand, but I can make them with a drewids head & the initials of your name or any other devices you please.

There was clearly further correspondence in the next six weeks which appears to no longer survive and in which it seems that Solomon tried to convince Boulton of the legality of the scheme and Boulton refused to be drawn into it. This becomes clear from a letter that Boulton eventually wrote to Thomas Williams himself on 15 September 1796. The first page is taken up with details of costings for (unspecified) items which Williams had asked Boulton to price. The second page then begins

---

99   Letter, Dr Solomon to Matthew Boulton, 29 July 1796 (MBP, MS 3782/12/41/231).

> I have long wished to see you at Soho & to communicate to you sundry letters which I have received from a D[r]. Soloman of Liverpool who wanted me to Coin for him exact Copys of your Anglesey pence and halfpence. He assures me he has taken Councils opinion upon the Legality of it & urged various arguments to induce me to undertake his order but my last letter has silenced him however. I hope you will contrive to dine with me or take your Bed as you go to Town & then I will show you the Correspondence.[100]

Legally, of course, Solomon was quite correct. The counterfeiting of tokens was not forbidden by law; indeed, the tokens were themselves technically illegal since a 1672 ban on their production and use was still in force, although it was everywhere ignored.[101] It was up to the token issuer to pursue his case in the civil courts.

Counterfeiting is as old as coinage itself, so Boulton was never going to win his war with the counterfeiters. Hopefully, however, this account of some of the skirmishes he fought with them has cast some fresh light on the man and his motivations and explains part of the fascination that coining held for him.

---

100 Copy letter, Matthew Boulton to Thomas Williams, 15 September 1796 (MBP, MS 3782/2/73/Item 123).
101 Selgin, *Good Money*, p.144. See M. Dickinson, *Seventeenth Century Tokens of the British Isles and their Values*, London, 1986, p.5, for the 1672 ban.

Chapter Two

Trading in Liberté: the commercial token and medal coinage of the Monneron Frères

Peter Jones

Matthew Boulton's interest in the lucrative potential of coining probably dates back to the earliest days of his partnership with James Watt. Coining was already an established cottage industry in Birmingham after all, and the technology involved in rolling and impressing copper varied little whether it was used to create buttons, coins or medallions. That Boulton considered the possibility of harnessing the power of steam to the action of the screw-press as early as 1774 is less certain. Yet there seems to be no good reason to doubt James Watt's later recollection that his partner did indeed raise this very question.[1] Even before James Watt's arrival in Birmingham, the application of steam for mechanical purposes had been a topic of conversation among the men who would coalesce to form the Lunar group. Erasmus Darwin broached the subject of steam-powered carriages with Boulton, and in 1768 he reported to the potter Josiah Wedgwood that a mutual friend, Richard Lovell Edgeworth, had actually come close to building such a vehicle.[2] It is beyond question, however, that Boulton took no action to modify the traditional technology associated with coining before 1787. There were many more promising applications for steam with more tangible money-making prospects. Coining can never have been far from his thoughts, though. We know that he was on the look out for markets for his strip copper on the continent of Europe because in 1784 he discussed with one of his Paris commercial contacts the possibility of tendering for

---

1   On this subject, see R. Margolis, 'Matthew Boulton's French Ventures of 1791 and 1792: Tokens for the Monnerons Frères of Paris', *British Numismatic Journal*, 58, 1988, p.102; R. Doty, *The Soho Mint & the Industrialization of Money*, London, 1998, pp.24-5, and the remarks of G. Selgin, *Good Money: Birmingham Button makers, the Royal Mint, and the Beginnings of Modern Coinage: Private Enterprise and Popular Coinage*, Oakland (California), 2008, p.62.

2   D. King-Hele (ed.), *The Collected Letters of Erasmus Darwin*, Cambridge, 2007, pp.64-4, pp.68-4.

the supply of copper to the mint at Limoges.[3] The idea may have germinated out of an earlier correspondence of a philosophical nature with Balthazar-Georges Sage, the chemist, mineralogist and assayer, who held a post at the Paris Mint. At all events Boulton was certainly coining for the East India Company in 1786, albeit in London rather than Birmingham, and by that date further discussions had undoubtedly taken place about the advantages of steam as a source of motive power.

The turning-point came later that year when the two partners visited Paris at the invitation and expense of the French government. They travelled in the capacity of consulting engineers whose ostensible purpose was to advise on the refurbishment of the Machine de Marly – that is to say the antiquated system of waterwheels and forcing pumps that raised water from the river Seine downstream from the capital in order to supply the royal palaces of the neighbourhood of Versailles. However, there were lots of other commercial irons in the fire – on both sides – and one of Boulton's chief objectives was to inspect, and profit from, the technological expertise of the Paris Mint. It was by this route that he was able to establish a personal friendship not only with a number of France's most eminent Academicians such as Sage, but also with Augustin Dupré and Jean-Pierre Droz, two of the most talented die-sinkers and copper-plate engravers of their generation. Jean-Pierre Droz seems to have gone out of his way to cultivate Matthew Boulton and James Watt during their seven week sojourn in Paris and it is not difficult to guess the reason why. As a new comer to coining Boulton was in the market for technological knowledge, whereas Droz was on the look-out for employment and preferment from France's first minister, Charles-Alexandre de Calonne. Since Calonne had invested hugely in Boulton and Watt's visit, both in a ministerial and in a personal capacity, it is likely that Droz felt that encouraging and accommodating the Birmingham button manufacturer in his coining ambitions was a safe two-way bet.

What neither party allowed for, however, was the unpredictable motions of the wheel of political fortune. Within three months of Boulton's return to Soho, Calonne had fallen from power. Under threat of impeachment, indeed, he found refuge in London and all the ambitious schemes of the previous winter were thrown into the melting pot. Matthew Boulton, too, had reason to believe that he had been dealt a poor hand by fate, for the illness of King George III put plans for a British regal copper coinage on hold. Even once the king had begun to recover his wits at the start of 1789, it would become apparent that the shortage of small change was scarcely the question occupying the forefront of Prime Minister Pitt's

---

3   Birmingham Central Library (hereafter BCL) MS 3782/12/29 Pradeaux to M. Boulton, Dunkirk, 18 April 1784.

mind. However, by this date Boulton had committed himself to a course of action from which it would have been difficult to withdraw. At vast expense he had retained the services of Jean-Pierre Droz, the Paris engraver who had dangled the prospect of an improved coining technology under his nose the year before, and he had given orders for the construction of a mint building on a site close by the Soho Manufactory. From the outset this building was designed to accommodate presses and cutting-out equipment powered by steam, and it was largely finished by the end of 1788. However, fitting it out with machinery capable of the rapid and continuous striking of coins with minimal manual intervention or effort proved a more arduous process. It pushed up the Soho 'bill account' (overdraft facility) to levels not seen since the late 1770s. In May 1789 James Watt reported to the Milanese natural philosopher, Marsilio Landriani, who had paid a highly successful visit to Soho the previous year that the presses were almost complete. But this was far from being the case in reality. The 'lap engine' which provided the power to cut out the blanks was not installed until the following month, and even then only one of the eight coining presses proved capable of working under steam power. Not until mid-1790 would the idea kindled many years earlier of a fully steam-powered mint reach fruition. By this date, however, the whole installation which included an upgraded rolling mill, two engines and an annealing stove, as well as presses had cost Boulton upwards of £5,000.

Unlike Watt, or for that matter Fothergill, his partner in the 1770s, Matthew Boulton was not a man to flinch from expenditure. Nevertheless, possession of a minting facility equipped with eight noisy, inefficient, yet serviceable, steam-powered presses, but no coining orders was an awkward situation to say the least. The economics of coining, as he must have realised, were quite different from the economics of button making. The capital requirement was considerable, demand spasmodic and the cost advantages of scale which it was assumed would flow from mechanisation and automation could only be achieved on the basis of very large orders. Striking tokens for the region's manufacturers and trading companies, or fashion medals for metropolitan consumers and collectors, might keep the facility ticking over, but it scarcely justified the initial investment. It is in this setting that we need to place the order from Monneron Frères of 1791. However, it is helpful to start with a preliminary look at the broader context of the industrial economy of the West Midlands.

In 1786 and 1787 Birmingham and the satellite towns of what would become known as the Black Country and the Potteries were gearing up for a huge expansion of trade to the Continent. In Britain and France negotiators were putting the finishing touches to a long-mooted commercial treaty, and it was widely assumed that multi-lateral agreements to liberalise trade across Europe would follow in its wake. Indeed, the visit of Boulton and Watt to Paris formed a part of this process, and the partners returned home with a healthy respect for the attention which the Bourbon government of France was now bestowing on industrial policy. Calonne's fall and the outbreak of revolution two years later did not alter this situation, at least not immediately. On the contrary, these events stimulated the commercial reflexes of Britain's most fleet-footed entrepreneurs. Matthew Boulton poured goods into France and Josiah Wedgwood did likewise. The creation of regiments of National Guardsmen throughout France from the summer of 1789 onwards inflated orders for troop uniform buttons, thereby ensuring that every fly-press in the West Midlands would be employed to maximum capacity. In the meantime, the revolutionaries' anti-sumptuary legislation gave an equivalent boost to the buckle industry. As patriotic citizens handed in their silver shoe buckles to be melted down, the demand for copper and copper gilt replacements boomed as never before.

The Soho Manufactory could not have been better placed to cater for this sharp rise in demand for decorative metal wares, of course. However, Matthew Boulton's main concern was for his mint. Now that the engine business was on an even keel, it had become his technological 'hobby horse'[4] and would absorb the largest portion of his time and energy for the remaining decade or so of his active life. Yet the prospect of a regal coinage for Great Britain had receded and lean years beckoned with capital tied up in an under-used plant. Boulton set out to re-invent himself as a currency reformer who just happened to be in a position to solve the country's developing small change crisis as well. But in the meantime, and more prosaically, he touted for business – any business that would keep some of his presses in motion. We know that he investigated the possibilities of coining for Spain, France, Prussia and some of the small city states of Europe, not to mention the United States. Spain seemed to offer the best hope initially owing to the huge demand for coin from her colonies, but revolution in France transformed the situation in that country and it soon became the main focus of his attention. France, too, faced an exchange problem, but a highly complex one. As in Britain there existed a chronic shortage of low denomination coin which the country's seventeen provincial mints seemed unable or unwilling to address. Unlike Britain, however, privately struck commercial or 'token' coins had not appeared to fill the gap to any significant extent. To this inherited problem the revolutionaries added one of their own making, for they resolved that the new regime must, of necessity, have a new coinage. Whilst deliberating on this reform, other issues began to

---

4   See K. Morgan (ed.), *An American Quaker in the British Isles: the Travel Journal of Jabez Maud Fisher, 1775-1779*, Oxford, 1992, p.255.

intrude upon the debate: whether to rely on a fully convertible paper currency backed by the sales of property formerly belonging to the Church, and whether bell metal recovered from redundant monastic houses could be used to manufacture coin. In the meantime, as the politicians deliberated, the scarcity of small denomination metallic currency became more acute by the day.

With the benefit of hindsight it is apparent that Matthew Boulton's dealings with France involved three distinct proposals. He would supply one or more steam-powered mints, lock stock and barrel, and engage to install the engines, presses etc. as directed. Failing that, he would coin in Soho for the Constitutional Monarchy or, if that proved politically unconscionable, ship blanks to the Romilly copper works where they could be struck on French soil. But if none of these solutions proved feasible, he would deal with third parties and produce commercial (i.e. unofficial) token currency to order. Whether the Minister of Finances and the deputies comprising the National Assembly's Monetary Committee ever acknowledged that they had a problem in need of one of Boulton's 'solutions' must be open to doubt. The vast quantities of bell metal accumulating in government depots would surely provide raw material of the correct metallurgical specification (they were wrong) and, in any case, Jean-Pierre Droz who had by now returned to Paris issued assurances that the technology and expertise necessary for steam-powered coining was available on the deputies' own doorstep. Besides, Boulton had British competitors when touting for a French coinage contract, as his agent discovered soon after his arrival in Paris early in 1791.

The decision to embark on a commercial moneying venture in partnership with the Monneron brothers reflected both his failure to make headway with the politicians who were now in control of the political destinies of France and a final realisation that he was not going to secure a regal coining contract for Britain in the foreseeable future either. One detects, too, a degree of desperation as Boulton's gambles foundered one by one. In June 1791 the Monetary Committee of the French National Assembly closed off another avenue, declaring that it would not be legal to strike money from copper strip brought into the country from abroad. Yet the Monnerons were nothing if not respectable and resourceful French citizens.[5] His agent in Paris described them as three brothers who had made substantial fortunes in the French colonies of the East Indies. In fact, there were ten male siblings all told, and they hailed from the Calvinist bourgeoisie of Annonay in the Vivarais. As such they would have been well known to the Huguenot bankers and

---

5   An account of the public careers of the principal Monneron brothers and their wide-ranging commercial and banking interests can be found in J. Bouchary, *Les Manieurs d'argent à Paris à la fin du XVIIIe siècle*, Paris, 1942, volume III, pp.181-247.

merchant houses of London to whom Matthew Boulton often turned for advice on matters concerning the credit worthiness of overseas business customers. The three eldest brothers combined wealth with political influence for they had been chosen as deputies to the Estates General,[6] whilst their younger sibling, Joseph-François-Augustin, would be elected to its successor, the Legislative Assembly. Contact with Jean-Louis and Pierre-Antoine (respectively the second and third eldest brothers) was first made early in 1791, and at this juncture it seems that Boulton was hoping to make use of their influence to press for a mint order from the French government. By the summer, however, his business plan had undergone a significant shift, for he began to buy-in large quantities of cake copper on the Monnerons' account with a view to a free-lance commercial coinage. The mint was made ready with additional annealing facilities, and in August contractual terms were agreed. A month later Boulton sent over to France specimen copper coins of different weights and sizes for his new partners to inspect.

Although the issuing of commercial copper coins, or 'tokens', as a means of overcoming the shortage of legal tender was a widespread practice in Britain at this time and one which was officially tolerated, if not sanctioned, private-enterprise coining was not well developed in France. Even in the spring of 1791 when guild restrictions were swept away and the ownership of screw-presses ceased to be a matter for official regulation, few merchants and manufacturers followed the example of their counterparts across the Channel. Apart from the Monnerons, we know of no more than a dozen.[7] To judge from the frequency with which rather poor quality specimens appear at auction today, moreover, their output must have been meagre when compared to the Monnerons' venture. French collectors describe these tokens as 'pseudo-monnaie' as well they might, for that is exactly what they were – a kind of substitute money which was designed to overcome the same small change problem in France as prevailed in Hanoverian England.

It seems likely that Matthew Boulton and the Monneron Frères were aware from the outset of the questionable nature of their scheme to introduce an informal token coinage to France. James Watt, Boulton's engine partner who had watched the building of the mint with some trepidation, resolved to stay well clear

---

6   Charles-Claude Ange and Jean-Louis sat for the Third Estate from the outset in 1789 and they would be joined by Pierre-Antoine in 1791.

7   Trade tokens were issued by the following: Lefèvre-Lesage et Compagnie négociants à Paris; Clémanson et Compagnie à Lyon; Dairolant, Le Clech et Compagnie à Clermont de l'Oise; Boyère négociants à Paris; Brun bijoutier; Givry commerçant; la manufacture de porcelaine Potter, rue Crussol à Paris; la caisse métallique établie à Paris; Thévenon; Montagny.

of the whole venture. For a start, powerful politicians in France were never won over to the idea of an interim solution to the small change problem which involved the striking of a metallic substitute for coin of the realm. Indeed, the deputies continued to cling to the idea that small denomination coins could be struck, or cast, from bronze (bell metal), and a decree to this effect was given the Royal Assent early in 1791. It followed, therefore, that a great deal of consideration had to be given to the question of the design and inscription of the new tokens, and to whether they would be liable to import duty upon their shipment to a port of entry. Since the issuing of 'monnaie' was deemed a regalian right, in France no less than in Britain, it was felt safer to play on a

Fig 9. Obverse, copper médaille de confiance 2 sols, *1791 (Assay Office 144) (Reproduced courtesy of The Birmingham Assay Office).*

marketing ambiguity and to describe the tokens as 'médailles de confiance'. Once they had been sold at a profit, in other words, it would be left to the consumer whether to use them as decorative medallions, or as a medium of exchange. Nevertheless, the Monneron brothers found a powerful alibi for their enterprise in the rhetoric of the Revolution itself, and one which they took pains to highlight in the iconography of the first of the tokens to be issued. The '2 *sols* monnerons'[8] sent out from Soho towards the end of 1791 featured on the obverse a lapidary reference to article five of the Declaration of the Rights of Man (**Fig 9**).[9]

The significance of this reference would not have been lost on contemporaries, even if it seems a little obscure to us today. Richard Twiss an Englishman, who visited Paris the following year, penned a detailed description of the type of currency that was now circulating in the French capital. It included two well engraved tradesmen's tokens, he reported, which were said to have been struck in Birmingham. The smaller of the two carried on the reverse the inscription 'médaille de confiance de deux sols à échanger contre des assignats de 50L et au dessus,'[10] together with a

---

8   There were 20 *sols* in a *livre tournois*. A Paris washerwoman could expect to earn about 1 *livre* a day in 1791, whereas a skilled artisan would earn between 2 and 3 *livres*.

9   'La loi n'a le droit de défendre que les actions nuisibles à la société. Tout ce qui n'est pas défendu par la loi ne peut être empêché, et nul ne peut être contraint à faire ce qu'elle n'ordonne pas.' [The law ought to prohibit only actions hurtful to society. What is not prohibited by the law, should not be hindered; nor should any one be compelled to that which the law does not require].

10   Two *sol* token convertible into paper currency [*assignats*] bearing a face value of 50 *livres* or above.

pointed invocation of clause five on the obverse as mentioned above, which he abbreviated in translation to 'The law has the right of prohibiting only those actions which are hurtful to society.'[11] These tokens invited the 'confidence' or trust of the public, who were requested to accept them in lieu of tender bearing the image of the sovereign. Nearly all the evidence suggests that they were indeed highly acceptable – as money. In fact, Matthew Boulton soon began to send over much larger '5 *sols*' copper tokens which incorporated a finely executed engraving of the 'Pacte fédératif'[12] by Dupré as well. Whilst quibbling over the condition of the merchandise on its arrival in France, the Monnerons reported that they were able to retail the larger specimens at double their face value. They circulated in Paris, Lyon, Strasbourg, Nantes and several large towns of the south, both as commercial coin and as collectable emblems of the progress of the revolution (**Fig 10**).

It is not difficult to understand why the monneron tokens were popular, for low value specie was in desperately short supply in France during the autumn and winter of 1791-2. The first revolutionary Assembly had made scant headway in turning bell metal into small change, large quantities of bullion were being exported, and the

Fig 10. Obverse (top) and reverse (bottom), gilt médaille de confiance 5 sols, 1792 (Assay Office 142) (Reproduced courtesy of The Birmingham Assay Office).

paper notes – or *assignats* – issued in anticipation of the liquidation of the assets of the Church were only available in very large denominations. Even then, they were not intended for day-to-day transactions; not initially at any rate. Only with the proclamation of the Republic in the early autumn of 1792 would the *assignat* take on the characteristics of an official currency with denominations to suit every pocket. Until that date private individuals, companies and municipal authorities frequently resorted to the printing of unofficial notes of exchange known as *mandats* or *billets de confiance*, although their circulation was necessarily confined since they

11 R. Twiss, *A Trip to Paris in July and August 1792*, Dublin, 1793, p.10 n. 7.

12 The 'Pacte fédératif' evokes the Festival of Federation held in Paris on 14 July 1790 to mark the anniversary of the fall of the Bastille.

possessed no intrinsic value. Typical is the *billet de confiance* of the municipality of Saint Martin-de-Valamas, which would have been used to facilitate transactions taking place at the fairs of this market town in the south of France. The *billet de confiance* should be seen as a parallel to the Monnerons' *médaille de confiance*. Both were issued on trust and with the promise of convertibility. Both were tolerated as a *faute de mieux* solution to the problem of small change, and both would be repudiated once the revolutionaries had found the time to think through and implement their currency reforms (**Fig 11**).

Fig 11. Paper billet de confiance de cinq sols, St. Martin-de-Valamas, *1792 (private collection).*

We know that Matthew Boulton struck all of the 2 and 5 *sols* monnerons using the steam-powered presses he had installed at Soho. Yet, as several researchers have pointed out, this was not a straightforward exercise and nor did it provide a ringing endorsement of the superiority of the 'high tech' approach to coining. Determined to secure as big a profit margin as possible from the venture, the Monneron brothers tinkered repeatedly with the metallic weight and finish of the tokens and medals they commissioned from Boulton. Meanwhile, the need to respond to, or circumvent, French legislators' pronouncements on coining imposed a near constant round of design changes. Finally, the demands of mass production, particularly of the heavier 5 *sols* pieces, pushed Boulton's prototype mint to its technological limits, and beyond. An initial re-cutting of the master dies took place almost immediately, and it was driven by the need to update the token-medals. On 2 January 1792 the Legislative Assembly had decided to re-calibrate the 'era of liberty' so that it would begin at the start of each calendar year. As a result, 'l'an III de la Liberté' which had only begun on 14 July 1791 was truncated. Boulton received instructions to alter the exergues of both the 2 *sols* and the 5 *sols* to 'l'an IV de la Liberté' with immediate effect. The opportunity was taken to make other minor alterations to the inscriptions, too, and because the retail operation was proceeding so promisingly the Monneron brothers decided to risk a weight reduction in order that the strike per pound of metal could be increased.

However, buoyant demand from consumers and the accommodating principles of the Declaration of the Rights of Man were not enough on their own to make a success of the venture. Aware that Louis Tarbé, one of the government's most senior civil servants, was hostile to private-enterprise coining, the Monnerons trod warily. Boulton grew alarmed, in consequence, and demanded to know the reasons for Tarbé's hostility – the more so as the king had put him in charge of the Ministry of

Public Revenues. In February, at the Customs House of Rouen, there was an attempt to interfere with the influx of token-medals on the ground that they were dutiable merchandise. No doubt Tarbé lay behind the manoeuvre. The Monnerons managed to fight off this exercise of bureaucratic power through the courts, and in the meantime Tarbé was ousted from the ministry. However, late in April 1792, a timid move in the direction of lower denomination *assignats* appeared to signal a diminishing role for commercial money. The measure prompted a further round of anxious consultation between the partners, and it seems to have led to the decision to prepare fresh dies on which the reverse inscription was altered from 'médaille de confiance remboursable en assignats de 50# et au dessus' to the less contentious 'médaille qui se vend 5-sols à Paris'. Again, the opportunity was taken to reduce both diameter and weight in the new format. Comparison reveals, moreover, that the 2 *sols* tokens underwent a similar transition in terms of their reverse inscription (**Fig 10**).

By the spring of 1792 Boulton and the Monnerons had probably concluded that the tolerance accorded to token coins would not long endure, and that a multi-faceted commerce in commemorative medallions was by far the safer trade. Since the French declaration of war against the Habsburgs in April 1792 the direction of revolutionary politics had become quite unpredictable, and besides, Monneron Frères were getting into financial deep water. To meet their liabilities, Pierre, together with Charles and Louis – that is to say the brothers whose trading house was teetering on the brink of insolvency[13] – urged Matthew Boulton to switch production towards what they described as 'médailles de fantaisie' (decorative medallions). This was all very well, but Soho could not immediately re-tool to accommodate the many different medal types, weights and finishes which Augustin, the younger Monneron, would now rely on to save the enterprise from financial disaster. Gilded medallions (the type with the biggest profit margin) were labour-intensive; nevertheless, on 7 June, Boulton promised to make as many 'as my Button gilders can do, without stoping my Button manufactory.'[14] In fact he seems never to have kept up with the demand for decorative medallions, even at the bottom of the price range, as his business partners reproachfully pointed out. Two tons of mixed copper specimens per week had been mentioned, but in February 1792 Boulton would acknowledge that this output had yet to be achieved. There was another problem, too, for the striking of the medals raised political questions every bit as delicate as those surrounding the striking of *médailles de confiance*.

Monneron Frères initially envisaged an entire medallic series commemorative of the principal personages and events of the revolution. To this end they commissioned

---

13   Payments were suspended on 30 March 1792, see Bouchary, *Les Manieurs d'argent*, pp.218-19.

14   BCL MS 3782/12/9 Copy letter of M. Boulton to A. Monneron, Soho, 7 June 1792.

dies of Bailly, Lafayette, Mirabeau, Pétion and the Serment du Roi.[15] However, it appears that the only medals actually to have gone into mass production at Soho were the Serment du Roi and Lafayette, together with Rousseau and Hercules. Augustin Monneron, who had been appointed by French creditors to manage the trade when Pierre defaulted and disappeared, pressed Boulton to strike exceedingly light-weight specimens at 80 to the pound which he would then be able to sell on at 1 *sol* each. Whilst collectors only would buy a Mirabeau medal, a Lafayette or a Rousseau would sell in their tens of thousands, he predicted. Yet there was scarcely any prospect that the hard-pressed Soho Mint could manufacture on this scale, at least not when all the serviceable mills were engaged upon striking 2 and 5 *sols* token money. The best that Boulton could manage were bronzed and gilt Rousseau medallions priced wholesale at 2½d each. Even so, his medallic output was to be counted by the gross rather than by the thousand. In any case Augustin's commercial zeal concealed a poor understanding of the state of domestic politics. On 10 May 1792, he assured Matthew Boulton that demand for medals of General Lafayette would escalate as French forces embarked upon a spring offensive against the Austrians in Flanders. On the strength of this intelligence, sixty percent of the medals supplied by Soho in the first four months of the campaigning season were 'lafayettes'. Yet the General betrayed the revolution and, having failed to persuade his troops to march on Paris, in August he defected (**Figs. 12, 13, 14, 15**).

Fig 12. Obverse, copper Serment du Roi medallion, *1791 (Assay Office 147) (Reproduced courtesy of The Birmingham Assay Office).*

Fig 13. Obverse, copper Lafayette medallion, *1791 (Assay Office 150) (Reproduced courtesy of The Birmingham Assay Office).*

The original dies for the Mirabeau, Lafayette and Rousseau medallions had been engraved by Rambert Dumarest whom we know to have worked on commission for Boulton both in Paris and in Birmingham, whereas the Serment du Roi and the

---

15   The 'Serment du Roi' refers to the swearing of the oath of allegiance to the Constitution by Louis XVI on the Champ de Mars, 14 September 1792.

Hercules obverses were engraved in France by Augustin Dupré.[16] After the costly saga of Jean-Pierre Droz's employment at Soho, Boulton was extremely wary of having any engraver permanently on his payroll. Nevertheless, production quality and workmanship remained paramount considerations for all the parties. Soho, or rather Sheffield, steel was used in preference to any continental grade, and Augustin Monneron carefully scrutinised the inscriptions and edge markings for blemishes and inaccuracies that might impede the retailing operation. The rim inscription of the Lafayette medal lacked an accent on the *e* of 'patenté', he pointed out on 18 June 1792, and the words 'se vend' on the obverse had been run together. As for the proof Hercules, the circular inscription on the obverse ('les français unis sont invincibles / the French united are invincible') required re-sizing and re-spacing.[17] He would have been better employed keeping an eye on domestic Parisian politics, for in the second half of June it became clear that both public events and the private enterprises of commercial coiners were heading for a spectacular denouement.

Fig 14. Obverse, copper Rousseau medallion, 1791 (Assay Office 151) (Reproduced courtesy of The Birmingham Assay Office).

When the crisis engendered by the overwhelming evidence of Lafayette's culpability finally broke in Paris on 10 August 1792, Augustin Monneron had just returned from a business trip to Soho. In his absence draft legislation had been presented to the Legislative Assembly banning French citizens from coining, or having coined, *médailles de confiance* for commercial circulation. Equivalent legislation would

Fig 15. Obverse, copper Hercules medallion, 1792 (Assay Office 145) (Reproduced courtesy of The Birmingham Assay Office).

also curtail the experiment in *billets de confiance*. Some intimation of the precariousness of his position must have occurred to Augustin, because on quitting London on the 3 August he made a spur of the moment decision to leave behind the packing case of

---

16   See C. Saunier, *Augustin Dupré, orfèvre, médailleur et graveur général des monnaies*, Paris, 1894; R. Trogan and P. Sorel, *Augustin Dupré (1748-1833): graveur général des monnaies de France*, Paris, 2000.

17   BCL MS 3782/12/91 A. Monneron to M. Boulton, Paris, 18 June 1792.

medallions that Boulton had prepared for despatch. It contained an assortment of plain copper, bronzed and gilt specimens, two-thirds of which bore effigies either of Lafayette or of King Louis XVI swearing the oath of allegiance to the constitution (Serment du Roi). Whilst a decree specifically prohibiting the importation of decorative medals did not pass through the Assembly until a fortnight later, Augustin Monneron must have offered up a silent prayer to the Calvinist equivalent of his guardian angel on his return to the French capital. With Louis and the royal family incarcerated in the Temple prison and Lafayette a traitor in the hands of the Austrians, possession of such emblems had become an indictable offence, or worse. In fact he *was* arrested – albeit briefly – seemingly as a consequence of the introduction of house searches and the decree banning the circulation of imported medals.[18] As for Boulton, he was behind the flow of the political tide across the Channel, yet, ironically, in a position now to commence mass production. Ever the optimist, he wrote to offer his partner ten tons of medal blanks which could be made up as directed, adding 'I suppose in the present circumstances you would not have any Medalls of La Fayett struck …'[19] However, the game was up. On 3 September 1792 the Assembly moved to close down the operations of the commercial token coiners and distributors as well. A new official coinage beckoned and low denomination *assignats* would provide an interim medium of exchange.

The 2 and 5 *sols* monnerons continued to be used for day-to-day payments, notwithstanding the law and the mounting hostility of the *sans-culottes* [20] to any form of specie which competed with the *assignat*. Indeed, they continued to be unloaded from vessels onto the quays of Dunkirk for onward despatch.[21] Not until the very end of 1793 or early 1794, it appears, did they disappear altogether from circulation. Matthew Boulton finally wound up his dealings with the Monnerons in March 1794 and, in the process, both sides suffered a significant financial loss. Nevertheless, some 183 tons of copper strip had been wrought into tokens and medals in less than a year.[22] Even if we allow that the Monneron coinage was not the only large order handled by Boulton's prototype mint, the fact remains that he managed to strike well over seven million 2 and 5 *sols* copper tokens for France,

---

18 On 24 August 1792, by virtue of a warrant of the Paris Commune, and detained in the Abbaye – one of the sites of the September prison massacres; see Bouchary, *Les Manieurs d'argent*, p.220.

19 *Ibid.*, M. Boulton to A. Monneron, Soho, 20 August 1792.

20 Political militants, both male and female, who were drawn from the urban labouring and artisanal classes.

21 On the shipment of monnerons, see R. Margolis, 'Those Pests of Canals: a theft of Monneron Tokens intended for France', *The British Numismatic Journal*, 75, 2005, pp.121-31.

22 Margolis, 'Matthew Boulton's French Ventures', p.108 note 30.

several thousand medallions, and an unknown quantity of tokens and medals in silver and silver gilt between November 1791 and September 1792. This was no mean achievement, even if it pales alongside the production figures that would be achieved by the second Soho Mint established in 1798. This facility managed to coin eighty million pieces of money in the year 1803 alone.[23] Historians have tended to blur the histories of the first and second Soho Mints, helped no doubt by the uncharacteristic reticence of Boulton himself. Once the elusive regal coining contract had been secured in 1797 and all traces of the original mint installation had been obliterated the following year, he lost interest in celebrating his earlier technological successes. In any case, the Monneron coinage had been a chancy venture from the start, and a losing one to boot. In a note penned over a decade later, he remarked simply that his original 'Hôtel de Money' had been infernally noisy, yet it had produced 'some tons of copper money.'[24]

This neglect of the first mint and of the Monneron commercial coinage that demonstrated its capabilities is unfortunate. In place of a historiography which undoubtedly exaggerated the technological novelty of Boulton's initial attempt to pioneer improved coining machinery, we are offered instead an interpretation which throws doubt on his oft-repeated claim to have achieved a productivity break-through. According to George Selgin, 'Boulton's [first] mint wasn't up to the job' and the strikes required to coin the heavy 5 *sols* tokens 'almost tore Soho's presses to pieces.'[25] Yet he acknowledges that steam-powered presses, when they were working properly, were capable of extraordinarily rapid coining speeds. So much so, indeed, that they risked creating a technological bottleneck inasmuch as fast-acting blank feeder machines had to be designed to keep up with the rate of production. Richard Doty's verdict on Boulton's first mint is more nuanced, by contrast.[26] But even if we allow Selgin's conservative estimate that Soho, in 1789, could only manage to strike ten coins in the time it took the manually operated presses of the Royal Mint to strike six, the saving in labour in-put was considerable. After 1789 and despite frequent stoppages, moreover, strike rates improved significantly – even though the tokens would be struck in restraining collars. By January 1792 two presses were actually achieving a rate of forty-five (of the 5 *sols* coins) per minute. In other words, Boulton and his mint foremen were learning on the job. The painful experience of the Monneron commercial coinage became

---

23   BCL MS 3782/12/56 Copy letter of M. Boulton to J. Banks, 23 January 1804 [*nota*: there are several versions of this letter].

24   BCL MS 3783/12/48 Note of M. Boulton, December [?] 1803.

25   Selgin, *Good Money*, p.116.

26   Doty, *The Soho Mint*, pp.43-7.

a lesson in the gains to be had from integrated, if not yet fully automated, production techniques. Early in 1793, by which time Soho's first experiment in mass coin production for a European market had ground to a halt, the American industrial spy, Thomas Digges, reported to Thomas Jefferson that Matthew Boulton was 'by far the neatest & best Coiner & has a more excellent apparatus for Coining than any in Europe.' He added:

> the whole machine is moved by an improvd steam Engine which rolls the Copper, for halfpence <u>finer</u> than copper has before been rolld for the purpose of money – It works the Coupoirs or screw press's for cutting the particular pieces of Copper & coins both the faces <u>& edges</u> of money at the same time, with such superior excellence & cheapness of workmanship, as well as with marks of such powerful machinery as must totally prevent counterfeiting it.[27]

As David Symons's chapter in this book shows, Digges's assumption regarding counterfeiting was certainly misplaced, but the rest did not fall too far short of the mark.

---

27   See R. H. Elias and E. D. Finch (eds), *Letters of Thomas Attwood Digges (1742-1821)*, Columbia (South Carolina), 1982, p.443.

Chapter Three

How Matthew Boulton helped make Birmingham 'the art capital of the world'

Richard Clay

As Sue Tungate notes in her introduction, as well as making key contributions to Birmingham's civic life, Matthew Boulton founded one of the eighteenth century's largest manufactories at Soho where he managed the production and sale of high quality silver, Sheffield plate, ormolu, Birmingham toys, buttons, 'mechanical paintings', and most famously, the world's first dual action steam engines.[1] But among Soho's diverse outputs, it was copper money that played the most crucial historical role in, to borrow a term from Tom Gretton, 'the massification' of art.[2] That is to say, copper money made at Soho was manufactured on an enormous scale and reached truly massive audiences. Indeed, one might argue that Boulton's minting activities helped make Birmingham the world's art capital in the 1790s and the first decade of the nineteenth century. Such a grandiose claim raises the question, 'does copper money made at Soho qualify as art?' But before offering an answer, I will first explore how 'massified' the copper money made at Soho was and the reasons for its production.[3]

---

1   Indeed, during Boulton's lifetime, his manufactory and its grounds became international and domestic tourist attractions for well-heeled travellers. Peter M. Jones, *Industrial Enlightenment: Science, technology and culture in Birmingham and the West Midlands 1760-1820*, Manchester, 2008, pp.95-100.

2   Tom Gretton, 'Clastic icons: prints taken from broken or reassembled blocks in some 'popular prints' of the Western tradition', Stacey Boldrick and Richard Clay (eds.), *Iconoclasm: contested objects, contested* terms, Aldershot, 2007, p.153.

3   I would like to thank the many people who helped me to research this chapter, who commented on versions of it given as lectures, and who helped me refine written drafts: Sally Baggott, Malcolm Dick, Richard Doty, David Dykes, Peter Jones, Val Loggie, Sian Roberts, David Symons, Sue Tungate, the staff and students of the History of Art departments of the University of Birmingham, the University of Bristol, the University of Edinburgh, members of the Lunar Society, members of the British Numismatic Society, and attendees of the AHRC-funded workshop series *Investigating and Communicating the Historical Significance of Matthew Boulton (1728-1809)*. Any errors of fact or interpretation are all my own work.

During the second half of the eighteenth century, enclosure of agricultural land in England allowed for increasingly mechanised and less labour intensive farming methods.[4] Growing numbers of people had little choice but to leave the countryside in search of employment in urban centres. Yet, wage differentials between town and country might have made such a move relatively attractive. While in 1793 Arthur Young estimated that the average agricultural wage in England was around 7s 6d per week,[5] in 1787 the *Birmingham Gazette* noted that a 'workman' in Birmingham received on average 9s or 10s per week.[6] Certainly, by 1792 the *Universal British Directory* estimated that Birmingham had a population of 60,000,[7] around eight times larger than in 1700.[8] Burgeoning urban wage economies generated unprecedented demand for low denomination coinage to pay employees and to provide change for the purchase of goods and services. Yet, between 1763 and 1770, the Royal Mint did not strike and distribute any halfpennies or farthings. A small issue of halfpennies was made between 1770 and 1775,[9] a limited issue of farthings followed in 1791,[10] then no copper coinage until 1797.

In the absence of adequate regal minting, the market for small change righted itself in two ways, the first of which, counterfeiting, is examined in detail by David Symons in this volume.[11] The legal alternative to producing fake regal coins was to revive the seventeenth-century practice of issuing unofficial tokens that functioned as low denomination money. Such a revival began on a large scale in 1787. Unlike counterfeit coins, tokens' iconography did not aim to convince the viewer that the objects were regal coins by resembling the latter visually. And, unlike official coinage, tokens were usually marked clearly with their nominal value, almost always a halfpenny or a penny, albeit a value higher than the exchange value of the metal from which the token was made. Importantly, those tokens which were produced in the largest numbers and entered wide circulation tended to bear text noting where

---

4   M. J. Daunton, *Progress and Poverty: An Economic and Social History of Britain, 1700-1850*, Oxford, 1995, pp.92-125. For a discussion of Matthew Boulton's involvement in land enclosures see: David Brown, 'Matthew Boulton, Enclosure and Landed Society' in Malcolm Dick (ed.), *Matthew Boulton (1728-1809): a Revolutionary Player*, Studley, 2009.

5   Witt Bowden, *Industrial society in England towards the end of the eighteenth century*, Macmillan, New York, 1925, p.219.

6   H. W. Dickinson, *Matthew Boulton*, Cambridge, 1937, p.139.

7   Anon, *Universal British Directory of Trade and Commerce and Manufacture*, London, 1792, p.202.

8   Peter Jones estimates Birmingham's population to have been between 7,000 and 8,000 in 1700. Jones, *Industrial Enlightenment*, p.34.

9   Richard Doty, *The Soho Mint and the Industrialization of Money*, London, 1998, p.3.

10 Dickinson, *Matthew Boulton*, p.135.

11 See pp.1-23 for Symons's chapter in this catalogue.

they could be redeemed, i.e. exchanged for an equivalent value of regal coin or goods.[12] As such, users could be relatively confident and, indeed, became increasingly so, that a bona fide token, unlike a counterfeit coin, ran little risk of being refused as payment at the point of exchange for goods or services.

The astonishing scale of the post-1787 production of tokens meant that the images imprinted on the objects' two faces were seen and owned by vastly larger and more diverse audiences than any other images of the era. After all, the principal means of mass producing high quality images in the late eighteenth-century was copper-plate etching. Yet, after 2000 impressions were made onto paper pressed against the copper plate, the metal would wear down and the diminishing quality of the resulting prints would render further copies increasingly hard to sell. Labour intensive production processes, coupled with relatively short production runs, meant that etchings were expensive and very few cost under a shilling – a significant proportion of the average labourer's more-or-less subsistence wages. Poorer quality woodcut prints, often appearing on, for example, ballad sheets, could cost a penny or less, thanks to the economies of scale allowed by wood's resilience. But woodcuts and etchings reached distinct markets with different spending power and varying aesthetic expectations. In contrast, audiences for any given token were enormously socially and culturally diverse. So, how big were these audiences – how 'massified' were tokens?

In 1801, Charles Pye, a copper-plate engraver from Birmingham, published a book about tokens that included 55 engravings depicting both sides of the objects he detailed in a list (**Fig 16**). Pye assured his readers that his acquaintance with Birmingham's producers of tokens meant that he could assert 'unequivocally' details about the numbers of such objects made in the town and he noted that 'more than three fourths of the […] tokens' were manufactured there.[13] George Selgin has estimated that something in the region of 600 tons of tokens were produced in Britain between 1787 and 1797 and,[14] by combining those figures with Arthur Waters' approximations of average numbers of tokens per lb and applying Pye's ratio,[15] one can conclude that over 46 million tokens were made in Birmingham in a single

---

12   In 1801 Charles Pye noted that some tokens, despite not bearing details of where they could be redeemed were, nevertheless, 'certainly made for circulation'. Charles Pye, *A correct and complete representation of all the provincial copper coins, tokens of trade, and cards of address, on copper, which were circulated as such between the years 1787 and 1801, when they were entirely superseded; a new coinage being at that time in circulation, issued by authority of the government*, London, 1801, p.4.

13   Pye, *A correct and complete representation*, p.3.

14   George Selgin, 'Steam, hot air, and small change: Matthew Boulton and the reform of Britain's coinage', *Economic History Review*, LVI, 3, 2003, pp.479-80.

15   See Arthur Waters, *Notes on Eighteenth Century Tokens*, London, 1954.

decade. Given the limitations of contemporary print making technology, it is clear that the post-1787 'token explosion' was by far the largest and most rapid influx of imagery into the public realm during the period and, perhaps, up until that point in history.

Tokens were issued in numerous towns across Britain, circulating throughout surrounding regions where they were accessible to members of any class engaged in transactions involving small change. Many of the tokens were issued by employers and used to pay employees. The first such large scale initiative was taken in 1787 by the 'copper king' Thomas Williams who owned mines in Wales, smelting works near Swansea and in Lancashire, and copper warehouses in Birmingham, Liverpool and London (see catalogue entry 8 for illustration). Like all tokens, authorship of the finished object was multiple. The prototype of what became known as the Anglesey penny appears to have been designed by one of Williams' associates, William Collins, and engraved by John Milton, in London.[16] The first issues might have been struck using Williams' own fly presses at Holywell but,[17] by the summer of 1787, production had shifted to Birmingham, using Westwood's presses and Hancock's die making skills.[18] Yet, in the same year, demand for the tokens was such that Boulton was asked to strike at least a couple of tons of them at the Soho Manufactory where, for reasons discussed below, a team of die sinkers

Fig 16. Charles Pye, Plate from Charles Pye, *'A correct and complete representation of all the provincial copper coins, tokens of trade, and cards of address, on copper, which were circulated as such between the years 1787 and 1801, when they were entirely superseded; a new coinage being at that time in circulation, issued by authority of the government',* copper-plate engraving, *1801 (Reproduced courtesy of The Birmingham Assay Office).*

---

16   I would like to thank David Dykes for clarifying the issue of authorship for me by allowing me to read a draft of part of his forthcoming book that is provisionally entitled, *Eighteenth-Century Provincial Coinage.*

17   C. R. Hawker, *Druid Tokens: eighteenth-century token notes from Matthew Boulton's letters,* Studley, 1996, pp.6-7.

18   Hawker, *Druid Tokens,* pp.9-11.

and press operators was being assembled.[19] Selgin has estimated that between 1787 and 1792 around 300 tons of Anglesey pennies and halfpennies were produced, marked as redeemable in Anglesey, London and Liverpool;[20] that is to say, around 20 million of these particularly heavy tokens.[21] Over 2 million were struck at Soho dated 1789 and 1791.[22] These are big numbers, given that Britain had a population of less than 10 million people at the time.

Also ordering tokens by the ton was the 'iron master' John Wilkinson who owned several Midlands iron works. Like Williams, he used tokens to pay his workers and made money out of having money made (**Fig 17**). Wayne Turner has argued that, having bought the copper and paid for the minting, each of Wilkinson's pennies cost him a little over half a penny.[23] Like the Anglesey pennies and halfpennies, Wilkinson's tokens were marked with places where they could be redeemed, initially his works in the Midlands – Willey, Snedhill, Bersham, and Bradley. However, they were certainly accepted further afield. Westwood of Birmingham designed dies for Wilkinson, sunk them, and used his and Williams' presses to produce tokens until production was shifted to Hancock in 1789. But by 1790 Wilkinson also needed to use the Soho team, writing to Matthew Boulton, as Turner notes, to say there

Fig 17. Obverse (top) and reverse (bottom), copper Wilkinson Forge halfpenny, 1792 (Assay Office 121) (Reproduced courtesy of The Birmingham Assay Office).

---

19   Hawker, *Druid Tokens*, pp.10-11.

20   Selgin, 'Steam, hot air, and small change', p.480.

21   To reach the estimate of 'around 20 million' I have taken into account that, while Waters works on the assumption that 103,040 tokens weighed an imperial ton, Anglesey halfpennies were unusually heavy compared to most other tokens and only 78,400 would equal a ton. Doty, *The Soho Mint*, p.303. I have rounded my estimate of the total number of Anglesey tokens down a little, bearing in mind that a significant number of them were the heavier pennies.

22   Doty, *The Soho Mint*, pp.303-304.

23   Wayne Turner, 'Wilkinson's trade tokens', *The Wilkinson Journal*, 7, 1979. It is worth noting that no evidence exists that the tokens discussed in this chapter were tied to use in shops owned by employers paying their workers in tokens, i.e. the tokens issued in the late-eighteenth century do not appear to have been part of a 'truck system'.

Fig 18 (left). Obverse (top) and reverse (bottom), copper Donald & Co halfpenny, *1792 (Assay Office 779) (Reproduced courtesy of The Birmingham Assay Office). Fig 19 (middle). Obverse (top) and reverse (bottom), copper* Birmingham Mining and Copper Company halfpenny and evasive halfpenny, *1791 (Assay Office 669 and 700) (Reproduced courtesy of The Birmingham Assay Office). Fig 20 (right). Obverse (top) and reverse (bottom), copper* Roe and Company Macclesfield halfpenny, *1789 (1968 N 332) and 1790 (1967 N 10) (Reproduced courtesy of Birmingham Museum and Art Gallery).*

was 'immediate demand' for 5 tons of tokens. By 1792, Wilkinson had moved all production to Boulton who, in due course, oversaw the manufacture of around 700,000 tokens.[24]

Numerous other employers also took to issuing tokens in the late 1780s and the early 1790s, including, for example, the 1792 halfpenny commissioned by stocking

---

24   Doty, *The Soho Mint*, pp.302-303. David Symons gives the slightly lower figure of 672,000 in D. Symons, 'Bringing to Perfection the Art of Coining', in S. Mason (ed), *Matthew Boulton: Selling what all the World Desires*, London and New Haven, 2009, p.91. Please note that in the cited essay by David Symons he notes his debt to a forthcoming publication by David Vice: D. Vice, 'A numismatic history of Soho Manufactory and Mint 1772-1850', *British Numismatic Journal*.

manufacturers Donald & Co in Birmingham (**Fig 18**), the 1791 Birmingham Mining and Copper Company halfpenny (**Fig 19**), and 1789 halfpennies struck for the copper concern Roe and Company in Macclesfield (**Fig 20**). In addition, numerous other tokens were issued in the name of whole towns. For example, at Soho there were struck almost half a million of the 1791 Glasgow Halfpenny (**Fig 21**), designed by the French die engraver, Rambert Dumarest, working for Boulton.[25] It was commissioned by the Glasgow employer – Gilbert Shearer & Co. In other cases, it is hard to know who commissioned town tokens, like the 1793 Birmingham halfpenny (**Fig 22**) which claimed around its edge to be 'current everywhere'. Working their way into wide circulation, many (although not all) employer and town tokens became common currency. Although tokens' circulation was often probably relatively localised, being widest in areas where cash wages were most commonly paid, the objects were, nevertheless, accessible across all classes of Britons. But, did the massive audiences for the images that tokens bore actually pay attention to the objects' iconography?

It is likely that people looked at tokens carefully, if only to check that the objects were trustworthy and not counterfeits, like the version of the Birmingham Mining

Fig 21 (far left). Obverse (top) and reverse (bottom), copper Glasgow halfpenny, *1791 (Assay Office 128) (Reproduced courtesy of The Birmingham Assay Office). Fig 22 (left). Obverse (top) and reverse (bottom), copper* Birmingham halfpenny, *1793 (Assay Office 692) (Reproduced courtesy of The Birmingham Assay Office).*

25   Doty, *The Soho Mint*, p.307.

and Copper Company Halfpenny (**Fig 19**) which bore the wrong name 'Birmingham *Coining* and Copper Company' and the word 'payable' but, unlike the original, no details of where.[26] Employers issuing tokens expected the objects to be examined by audiences. In 1801, Pye noted that some tokens were 'not made for circulation [...], but rather as substantial cards of address, pointing out the trade and residence of the issuer'.[27] But, arguably, all tokens that *were* made for circulation, as well as being a cost effective means of paying workers, also served as a means of publicity for a business, a hardwearing, widely disseminated, advert that associated the issuer with monetary value. Hence, the expense a patron like John Wilkinson was willing to go to, having dies designed and produced by skilled teams. Wilkinson was proud of the tokens, noting in a letter to Matthew Boulton in 1787 that everyone who had been shown the proofs for his first set had approved.[28] When he drafted that piece of correspondence, Wilkinson had probably not yet read the poem that appeared in *The New London Magazine* in December 1787 which, while demonstrating that people were indeed looking at the tokens, shows they were not necessarily doing so approvingly. It is worth bearing in mind that the only portrait to appear on contemporary regal coinage was the king's:

> In Greece and Rome your men of parts,
> Renown'd in arms or form'd in arts
> On splendid coins and medals shown,
> To make their deeds and persons known;
> So Wilkinson, from this example,
> Gives of himself a matchless sample!
> And bids the Iron monarch pass
> Like his own metal wrapt in Brass!
> Which shows his modesty and sense,
> And how, and where, he made his pence.

---

26 A legal case from 1787, reported by Hutton, indicates that people were well aware of the need to look carefully at coins to check for counterfeits. 'T. sent to C. desiring he would change half a guinea. This was by candle-light. In a few minutes after the messenger was gone, the half-guinea was suspected; the next morning it was visibly bad, and returned. T. alleged it was not his, for it was too bad for any man to take but a blind one.' W. Hutton, *Courts of requests: their nature, utility, and powers described with a variety of cases, determined in that of Birmingham*, Birmingham, 1787, p.108. While the aforementioned example pertains to a large denomination coin, one might suppose that people were also alert to whether their small change was, in Hutton's terms, 'visibly bad'.

27 Pye, *A correct and complete representation*, p.4.

28 Turner, 'Wilkinson's trade tokens'.

> As iron when 'tis brought in taction,
> Collects the copper by attraction,
> So, thus, in him 'twas very proper,
> To stamp his brazen face on Copper[29]

Not that Wilkinson was put off. In a letter to Boulton in February 1791 the 'iron master' was willing to sacrifice time and money to 'be plastered again',[30] i.e. to have a fresh plaster portrait produced that would be the basis for his likeness on a new edition of tokens. It might not be a coincidence that this 1791 issue of halfpennies bore on its reverse another new image, one that recalls the 1787 poem's reference to 'Greece and Rome'. The 1787 token and most of those of those of later years represented an iron worker holding metal under a trip hammer (**Fig 17**). That design contrasts with the 1791 reverse which elevates the ironworker to the status of a heroically nude classicised Vulcan (**Fig 23**).[31] Perhaps this version was a *riposte* to the magazine, showing that Wilkinson's pride lay in his workers' achievements as well as his own.

Nowadays, most people pay scant attention to the coins in their pockets. But might eighteenth-century employers have assumed that employees would consider tokens' iconography rather more closely, given that images were populuxe goods for workers living near the bread line? Were employers who issued tokens, using the objects to communicate meanings to their staff? If so, goodness knows whether Wilkinson's workers interpreted the 1791 Vulcan as a heroicising compliment to them or as a vainglorious claim about Wilkinson's own status. It is also impossible to know for sure what they made of the trip-hammer tokens, almost certainly the first images they owned of people like themselves at work (**Fig 17**). But, by applying the basic visual rhetoric of

Fig 23. Reverse, copper Wilkinson Vulcan halfpenny, 1791 (Assay Office 738) (Reproduced courtesy of The Birmingham Assay Office).

---

29 R. C. Bell, *Commercial Coins 1787-1804*, Newcastle, 1963, p.145.

30 Turner, 'Wilkinson's trade tokens'.

31 I would like to thank David Dykes for pointing out that Hancock based his design for the figure of Vulcan on an antique cornelian in Joseph Spence, *Polymetis: or, An Enquiry concerning the Agreement Between the Works of the Roman Poets, And the Remains of the Antient Artists. Being An Attempt to illustrate them mutuall from one another*, London, 1747, book 1, 80 and Plate X. Dykes notes that Spence's Vulcan was, in turn, derived from Leonardo Agostini, *Le gemme antiche figurante*, Rome, 1657, volume 1, Plate 118.

relative size, the employees could have concluded that the trip-hammer operator is tiny in comparison to Wilkinson's portrait, a size differential that connotes the power relations between the semi-regal paymaster and the waged worker who is dwarfed by the owner's capital goods. It was those depicted power relations that meant the images themselves arrived in workers' hands as pay. As such, the token can be interpreted as having a distinct ideological function. It represented as normal the capitalist wage relationship that was emerging to dominance and that Marxists would later argue is always unfair because the value of labour to the employer is never equal to the value of the wage awarded to the labourer.

Many other employers who issued tokens commissioned imagery that represented positively the relationship between work and wages. For example, Roe and Company's halfpennies used a female allegory bearing what Pye described as symbols of the 'principles of mechanics', thus alluding to the kind of labour that earned the company's workers their payment in the form of the tokens (**Fig 20**).[32] The reverse of the Donald & Co token (**Fig 18**) featured a beehive which Pye decoded as 'industry through which [people] acquire wealth' – wealth in the form of tokens. The Birmingham Mining and Copper Company (**Fig 19**) tokens bore an image of a female allegory holding fasces, representing strength through unity. The only apparent reference to the labour involved in copper mining might be the rock upon which the figure sits. However, the reverse emphasises the rewards of labour as signified by the symbol of wealth – an over-flowing cornucopia – upon which stands a stork. The latter is usually a symbol of vigilance but, perhaps in this context, is better understood as connoting the focused effort that generates wealth. Some other tokens used text to anchor the meanings of their visual symbolism, for example, the 1793 Birmingham halfpenny (**Fig 22**). It was not issued by any particular employer, but might have found its way into the hands of the workers employed in the town's mechanical trades.[33] On the obverse we see an almost naked allegorical boy holding a spanner and leaning on an augur, symbolising mechanical work. On the reverse the text states that 'INDUSTRY HAS ITS SURE REWARD' – rewards granted in the form of the object itself, i.e. halfpennies paid as wages.

While it is extremely difficult to know the extent to which the iconography of tokens would have been intelligible to many of the objects' potential audiences, it was probably readily recognisable. Hence, imagery used on tokens featured prominently in a poster that was first printed in 1792 to advertise the Soho Manufactory's insurance scheme to Boulton's socially diverse workforce (**Fig 24**). Employees unable

---

32   Pye, *A correct and complete representation*, p.7 (footnote).

33   It is possible that this was a 'specious token', i.e. one that claimed to be 'current everywhere' but which is not marked as actually being redeemable anywhere.

Fig 24. Anon, From Art, Industry, and Society, Great Blessings flow, *etching, (Reproduced courtesy of the Birmingham Assay Office).*

to read the detailed text which often accompanied the image could still recognise a worker with his arm in a sling, seated in the grounds of the manufactory in which they worked. The allegorical figure who holds the worker's hand is pointing to the bottom right foreground of the image which contains a series of symbols common on the tokens that all Soho workers would receive regularly in their small change: beehive, cornucopia, stork, symbols of mechanics like screws. Regardless of whether the viewer could fully decode a relatively complicated allegory, surely, they could grasp the poster's key message which was, 'reading' the image from left to right, 'at Soho workers who are incapacitated are treated well; they still get money'. Using symbolism disseminated by millions of tokens, the poster, like the tokens, helped to reinforce the ideological construction of wage relations' justness and, in this case, their particular fairness at Soho. In reality, the insurance scheme might be construed as less benevolent than it ostensibly appeared. Until 1804, no Soho worker could leave the manufactory and take with them the money they had contributed to the compulsory scheme, even if it had never paid out to them. As such, the scheme can be seen as serving as a means of keeping skilled workers earning wages at Soho.[34]

---

34   Eric Roll, *An early experiment in industrial organisation being a history of the firm of Boulton and Watt, 1775-1805*, London, 1930, p.229.

Certainly, it was in Boulton's interest not to lose his staff. The poster itself alludes to investment in their training. The explanatory text that often accompanied the image on the poster explained the figures in the right middle-ground as being 'little Boys busy in designing &c., which shew that an early Application to the Study of Arts, is an effectual Means to improve them'. Visually, the print alludes rather explicitly to the division of the arts in the left foreground motifs of cog wheel and screw (mechanical arts) located behind a painter's palette and a manuscript (liberal arts). As such, the etching echoes dominant views of the arts' sub-divisions as expressed in the third edition of William Henry Hall's *The new encyclopaedia*, published in 1797. Referring to Francis Bacon, it said that the 'arts' were 'commonly divided into the useful or mechanical' and the 'liberal and polite'. The former involved the hand more than the mind and they 'furnish us with the necessities of life', while the latter were 'the labour of the mind more than of the hand' and their end was 'pleasure'.[35] Yet, the text of the insurance poster emphasises the inter-connectedness of the mechanical and liberal arts, noting that a figure of 'Art' 'looks up to Minerva, Goddess of Arts'. Visually and textually, the poster connoted both the interdependence of, and distinction between, the mechanical and liberal arts at Soho. Like other products produced there, tokens were, in eighteenth-century terms, the outputs of both the mechanical *and* the liberal arts. They required the labour of the hand *and* the mind, resulting in a product that was a necessity in the cash and wage economy but also a source of pleasure – and there is ample evidence that considerable audiences regarded tokens primarily in the latter terms.

In his first book on tokens, published in 1795, Charles Pye noted that 'The great variety of Provincial Copper Coins issued between the years of 1787 and 1794 induced many people to make collections of them'.[36] The book's text is short, the vast majority of the pages being 36 copper plate engravings. But, Pye did find space to comment on the quality of execution of the tokens, an aesthetic judgement that invites parallels with contemporary discourses on the liberal arts. In 1796, Samuel Birchall went further in, *A descriptive list of the provincial copper coins or tokens*. He referred to the collector as a 'Virtuoso'.[37] In 1798, James Conder's, *An Arrangement of Provincial Coin, Tokens, and Medalets* was published in Ipswich and it noted a series of recent articles on related subjects in the *Gentleman's Magazine*, marking a further

---

35   William Henry Hall, *The new encylopaedia; or, modern universal dictionary of arts and sciences, on a new and improved plan. … In three volumes. By William Henry Hall, Esquire. The third edition. Revised, corrected, and enlarged, with considerable additions, improvements and modern discoveries, by Thomas Augustus Lloyd, … Illustrated with upwards of one hundred and fifty superb copper-plates*, Vol. 1, 1797, p.372.

36   Charles Pye, *Provincial copper coins or tokens, issued between the years 1787 and 1796, engraved by C. Pye, of Birmingham, from the originals in his own possession*, Birmingham, 1795, unpaginated.

37   Samuel Birchall, *A descriptive list of the provincial copper coins or tokens, issued between the years 1786 and 1796*, Leeds, 1796, unpaginated.

move towards the growing aesthetic focus of writing about tokens. The author of Conder's introduction, James Wright, claimed that the study of tokens, coins and medals by collectors meant that people had 'extended their knowledge' and 'refined their taste' – elevating their minds and bringing them pleasure.[38] His examples of earlier collectors indicates the role that such activities had in marking social distinction for their latter day equivalents; he listed: 'Charles I. and II, Cromwell, the great painter Rubens, the sublime artist Michael Angelo, Jameson the Vandyck of Scotland, the accomplished Sir Hans Sloane'. Not that collecting was necessarily straightforward. Wright tells of a Monsieur Vaillant, 'During one of his voyages into Greece, made for the purpose of collection, in returning to Marseilles, a corsair appeared in sight of the vessel which bore him. M. Vaillant, alarmed for his treasure, speedily selected and swallowed twenty of his most beautiful Greek coins. A change of wind, however, relieved him from his anxieties; and the fond antiquary, after suffering much distress from several ounces of ancient metal, recovered the pieces in a natural manner in the neighbourhood of Lyons.' Of course, collecting tokens issued recently in Britain was safer and cheaper than aping Vaillant's antiquarianism.

Wright placed on a par a collector's focus on old and new objects. He wrote that, 'Taken collectively, ancient and modern, they form the most numerous, the most various, the most valuable, the most durable, and, perhaps, in some instances, the most exquisitely finished of any class of the productions of human invention'. He went on to add that provincial tokens 'some of them being of interesting design and elegant execution [have] very much attracted the attention of lettered medallists, and gentlemen of taste in the arts'. He described tokens as 'among the best productions of modern art' and situated them squarely as an 'elegant art'. Wright and a series of other authors were catering for diverse audiences involved in what Thomas Spence's 1795 book on tokens described as, a 'universal rage of collecting coins'.[39] Even if one accepts Wright's proviso that two thirds of tokens were 'degraded' (presumably meaning not aesthetically good), like other writers addressing collectors, he was discussing tokens as if they were categorisable as liberal art objects – products of intellectual as well as manual labour, provoking thought and pleasure. Given the

---

38   James Wright, 'Preface' in James Condor, *An Arrangement of Provincial Coins, Tokens, and Medalets Issued in Great Britain, Ireland, and the Colonies Within the Last Twenty Years' from the Farthing to the Penny Size*, Ipswich, 1798, unpaginated.

39   Thomas Spence, *The coin collector's companion. Being a descriptive alphabetical list of the modern and provincial, political and other copper coins*, London, 1795, unpaginated. As well as being a numismatic author and dealer, Spence was a radical reformer who was arrested several times (once for selling Thomas Paine's, *The Rights of Man*). The Barber Institute exhibition that this book accompanies, *Matthew Boulton and the art of making money*, displays a regal coin counter-stamped, no doubt by Spence himself, with 'Spence's Plan', promoting his proposals for the reform of land ownership.

views of such authors and their readers, and given the sheer scale of token production in Birmingham in the decade and a half after 1787, it seems reasonable to assert that, at least in quantitative terms, the town *was* the world's art capital, especially if one considers activity at the Soho Mint not as yet mentioned in this chapter.

As Peter Jones' chapter in this book shows, Boulton established Soho's mint in order to develop technology that would allow him to solve the shortage of small change in one fell swoop. He wanted to produce new regal coin. By 1789 his company's early use of traditional fly presses was being abandoned in place of steam driven presses developed by a team of his work's engineers. He claimed his equipment, run by two boys, could produce 40,000 tokens an hour.[40] Importantly, in 1788, Boulton had also succeeded in buying in the expertise of a highly esteemed Swiss die engraver employed at the mint, La Monnaie, in Paris, Jean-Pierre Droz.[41] Droz had designed a collar which, when drastically improved by Boulton's team, allowed for the production of coins of precisely the same size and with straight edges that could be stamped in the same single, efficient movement as the obverse and reverse sides. It was very hard to counterfeit such objects to exactly the same dimensions, in such shallow relief, and with the unparalleled neatness of edge inscriptions. Lawson had invented a mechanism that, working with the improved Droz collar, separated the impressed blank from the die onto which it had been crushed by the press, speeding up production.[42] Boulton's team subsequently worked out a way to feed blanks into steam presses mechanically.[43] These technical innovations were combined with Droz's brilliant engravings which Boulton and many others considered to be all but peerless in Europe. The detail of Droz's shallow relief designs would be hard for lesser engravers to counterfeit.

Importantly, the aesthetic quality of Droz's designs was fine enough for Boulton to take them in 1788 to the Privy Council, to parliamentary friends, even to seek their presentation to the King and Queen at court, arguing that he could produce fine coins cheaply and on a massive scale (see catalogue entry 16). Although the coins would be in a base metal (albeit, unusually, worth the object's nominal value), the finished article would be so fine a product of the liberal arts as to warrant bearing the king's likeness. As Pollard has shown, the proofs were so impressive that Benjamin West, the President of the Royal Academy, entered into correspondence with Boulton in 1788, agreeing to help Droz gain a better likeness

---

40 Rev. Stebbing Shaw, *The history and antiquities of Staffordshire*, London, 1801, vol. 2, p.118.

41 J. G. Pollard, 'Matthew Boulton and J.-P. Droz', *The Numismatic Chronicle*, Volume VIII, 1968, pp.244.

42 Pollard, 'Matthew Boulton and J.-P. Droz', p.247. It was 1790 before Boulton's team managed to use steam driven presses to mint tokens using collars. Selgin, 'Steam, hot air, and small change', p.481.

43 Dickinson, *Matthew Boulton*, p.142.

of George III through reference to West's own portrait of the monarch and those by Gainsborough. Coining was work worthy of assistance from Britain's most senior liberal artist. As Dr Lind wrote in a letter to Boulton on 2 July 1788, having impressed West was important because 'he is the man that guides taste [...], his taking an active part in the business will be of no small advantage to your scheme.'[44]

It was not until 1797 that Boulton secured the contract for, and began to mint, regal pennies and twopences. By then, Boulton and Droz had parted ways and the entrepreneur had employed and released two other die engravers, Dumarest and Ponthon who had built their reputations in Paris. But Boulton had used his network of correspondents in Europe to recruit to Soho a German die engraver Conrad Heinrich Küchler. He was the designer of the coins that, for obvious reasons, became known as 'Cartwheels' (see catalogue entry 17 for illustration). The reverse bore the first depiction of Britannia with a trident instead of a spear, a motif which, along with the ship riding the waves behind the allegory, represented Briton as a maritime power at a time when it was competing with France to rule the waves. Given the invasion threat from revolutionary France, and the massive militia movement and military recruitment campaigns building in Britain, it was a particularly timely moment to circulate on an enormous scale a portable symbol of national identity that every Briton would come to know and recognise.[45] In one fell swoop, Boulton's team offered Britain a shared symbolic currency of national identity. But were the cartwheels considered to be art?

Certainly, Küchler was highly esteemed by some of his contemporaries. Wright rated a medal designed by Küchler as being comparable, maybe even equal, to the best antique coins.[46] In a letter to Boulton dated 1 September 1797, Wright described the 'cartwheel' as being 'by far the most elegant coinage that was ever actually brought into circulation by government at any period of British History'. He added that, 'the whole figure and design with the strong execution of Britannia on the Reverse are all admirable and perhaps scarcely permit of any improvement.'[47] On the other hand, as Pollard has noted, a leading die engraver at La Monnaie in Paris told one of Boulton's agents that Küchler was a 'mere

---

44   Pollard, 'Matthew Boulton and J.-P. Droz', p.260.

45   I think that the outline of the figure of Britannia resembles that of the British Isles, the lines of the Union Jack on her shield intersect where the country's capital lies, her back is turned on the Continent, and she holds the olive leaf aloft over Ireland (soon to sign the Act of Union).

46   James Wright, 'Preface', unpaginated.

47   Boulton and Watt Archive, MS 3782-12-42, item 215. I would like to thank Sue Tungate for locating this reference, transcribing it, and passing it on to me so generously.

mannerist'.[48] Yet, the status of Küchler's coins as liberal art in the late-1790s seems to be corroborated, not only by these aesthetic disputes, but also by the debates around the designs for a further batch of coinage.

When the Privy Council's committee, convened to discuss a new issue of regal currency, on 19 July 1798, they had called in a delegation of senior Royal Academicians (RA). West, Bacon, Smirk and Lawrence were asked to consider 'the improvements to be made in the fashion of the new coin' and to 'prepare drawings or models'.[49] On 20 December 1798, the RA delegation attended the committee's meeting and presented designs none of which were the delegates' own work. The minutes record the Lords saying that they 'would have been glad to have found among their Drawings and Models, some of the Productions of Men so eminent for their Talent, as the Gentlemen who composed the Committee of the Royal Academy' – that is to say, the delegates themselves.[50] The Councillors went on to criticise the designs that had been submitted, saying 'some of the most ancient Gold coins of this Realm had borne the Device of a Ship, which in a Country so renowned for Naval Exploits, and for its far extended commerce, was at all times, and particularly in the present Moment of great naval Success and Glory, to be considered as a very appropriate device'.[51] Clearly, the Privy Council was after the highest quality liberal art by the most senior RAs and in the form of designs that communicated patriotic meanings with the kind of contemporary resonance displayed by early British coins and, I note, by Küchler's 'Cartwheels'.

The diary entry of Joseph Farington RA for 16 March 1799 noted that all the senior members of the Royal Academy's delegation were, finally, ready to deliver designs of their own to the Privy Council.[52] The Council's minutes then went quiet about the RA's contribution. However, Farrington's diary entry for Christmas day 1799 reported that the renowned RA sculptor Flaxman, 'spoke of the business of the coinage which has been conducted in a manner degrading to the character of the Royal Academy. – That body was applied to, – gave designs, yet with[ou]t. further communication the Privy Council have thrown the whole into the hands of Bolton [sic] of Birmingham.'[53] Whether Flaxman liked it or not, the aristocratic

---

48   J. G. Pollard, 'Matthew Boulton and Conrad Heinrich Küchler', *The Numismatic Chronicle*, X, 1970, p.265.

49   *Minutes of the Lords of the Committee of Council for Coin from 10th February 1798 to 22nd October 1802*, MS, The Birmingham Assay Office library, p.120.

50   *Minutes of the Lords of the Committee*, pp.169-170.

51   *Minutes of the Lords of the Committee*, pp.171.

52   Kenneth Garlick and Angus Macintyre (eds.), *The diary of Joseph Farington*, volume IV, London, 1979, p.1174.

53   Garlick and Macintyre (eds.), *The diary of Joseph Farington*, volume IV, p.1331.

arbiters of aesthetic quality in matters numismatic, that class of Britons so key as patrons and connoisseurs of RA-style liberal art, the very men who had called upon the RA for designs, had, in the end, plumped instead for the same Soho team responsible for the 'Cartwheel' design.

According to David Vice's estimates, by 1806 well over 257 million regal coins had been produced at Soho for domestic circulation (although some went to Australia and to the Cape Colony).[54] If to that figure we add my earlier estimate of 48 million trade tokens produced in Birmingham from 1787 onwards, including those at Soho, the city's presses turned out well over 300 million coins and tokens in little more than 20 years. And that is not counting the thousands of medals, or well over 200 million coins and tokens produced by Boulton for the East India Company, the Sierra Leone Company, Ireland, the Isle of Man, France, or the mint technology sold by Boulton to Russia and Denmark and eventually, installed at the Royal Mint in London and opened officially in 1812.

If it is the case that objects become art objects when nominated as such by certain groups of people, including artists, patrons, critics, collectors and connoisseurs, then the coins, as well as the tokens and medals, produced in Birmingham in the late eighteenth and early-nineteenth centuries were, in contemporary terms, art objects. And, albeit briefly, in quantitative terms Birmingham was the art capital of the world.[55] Given that late nineteenth-century advances in photo-mechanical reproduction meant that two-dimensional images came to dominate visual culture, it is striking to note that, during Boulton's lifetime, the global 'massification' of art actually took the form of shallow relief-sculptures. Soho's steam presses helped put three-dimensional art into the pockets of millions of people around the world, in the process aiding the emergence of a global cash economy. Boulton had established a team of mechanical and liberal artists from across Europe that together mastered the art of making money and, in the process, made a good deal of money for Boulton. Yet, this cosmopolitan endeavour ended up effectively removing from circulation a huge number of diverse images – the tokens first issued in 1787 began to be rendered obsolete by the 'cartwheel' issue of 1797. Tokens that had represented and constructed the diverse regional, class, gender, and trade-based identities of Britons were all but replaced by a single regal copper coinage. The common symbolic currency of British currency became nationalistic.

---

54 Cited in Symons, 'Bringing to Perfection the Art of Coining', p.95.

55 I suspect that even those people who might struggle to accept that coins and tokens can be categorised as 'art' would, nevertheless, accept that Birmingham's production of 500-600 million of those objects in scarcely more than two decades means that the town was the image-making capital of the world, at least in quantitative terms.

Chapter Four

Catalogue

Sue Tungate

This catalogue includes details of 'star objects' that were selected by the curatorial team from among more than 170 items displayed in the exhibition *Matthew Boulton and the Art of Making Money* held between 7 May 2009 and 16 May 2010 at the Barber Institute of Fine Arts (University of Birmingham).[1]

Key to catalogue entries: Measurements for a coin, medal or token are given in terms of the object's diameter in millimetres (mm). All objects' edges are plain, unless otherwise stated. Other measurements are given as height x width in millimetres (mm). All figures given for numbers of coins, medals, or tokens produced are taken from Vice.[2]

Abbreviations: BM: British Museum; BMAG: Birmingham Museum and Art Gallery; Assay Office: Birmingham Assay Office; BHM: British Historical Medals;[3] D&H: Dalton and Hamer.[4]

---

1   Unless otherwise stated, all of the 'star' coins, medals and tokens that are discussed in this catalogue were produced at the Soho Mint between 1772 and 1809. Most of the Soho production of coins, medals and tokens was in copper, but those shown here may be bronzed copper, gilt, silver, or gold samples produced for collectors. Given that many of the objects discussed in this catalogue are coins or tokens, it is worth noting that, during the eighteenth century, the guinea was used for large value transactions, though all monetary values were given in pounds (£), shillings (s) and pence (d). Most of the coins produced by Boulton's Soho Mint were pennies, halfpennies or farthings (1/4d). This system, with twenty shillings to the pound and twelve pennies to the shilling was retained until decimalisation of the regal coinage in 1971.

2   Minting numbers given throughout this catalogue are from an excellent monograph by David Vice (forthcoming British Numismatic Society Special Publication). I thank David for allowing me a preview of this outstanding piece of scholarship.

3   Laurence Brown, *A Catalogue of British Historical Medals 1760-1960, Volume 1: The Accession of George III to the Death of William IV Seaby*, London, 1980; see also Christopher Eimer, *British Commemorative Medals and their Values Seaby*, London, 1987.

4   R. Dalton and S. H. Hamer, *The Provincial Token-Coinage of the Eighteenth Century Illustrated* (in four volumes), London, 1910-1915.

BOULTON: THE MAN AND HIS MANUFACTORY

1. MATTHEW BOULTON MEMORIAL MEDALS

Matthew Boulton's son, Matthew Robinson Boulton (1770-1842), commissioned a memorial medal (BHM 976) to mark the 1809 death of his father. The medal was issued in 1819 and engraved by G. F. Pidgeon. It was given to colleagues such as James Watt, William Murdoch, Peter Ewart, John Rennie and to friends of Matthew Boulton (including Sir Joseph Banks, Dr Herschel, the Earl of Dartmouth) as well as the British Museum and the Royal Mint.[5] The inscription (from Virgil, *Aenid*, VI, 663) alludes to Boulton's contributions to the mechanical and liberal arts. This was a large and well made medal, but Edward Thomason, who had been an apprentice at Soho, went one better with another design for a medal. He wrote 'The respect and esteem which I hold in Memory of the Values and Talents of my late worthy Master Matthew Boulton Esquire induced me to Commemorate him on the largest Medal ever made'.[6] He sent the first example struck (BHM 660) to Sarah Sophia Banks.[7] Several other memorial medals were made in honour of Matthew Boulton. One such medal, bearing his bust (BHM 661) and, on the reverse Farewel (sic), is rare, as are the 530 *Obsequies* (BHM 662) medals that were presented to Boulton's workmen at his funeral.

1819 Pidgeon Memorial Medal (BHM 976) Assay Office 55. 64mm; 100g plus; bronzed. Engraver: Pidgeon.

---

5   MS 3782-73-37 Item 117, 30 September 1820. (All MS references are from the Birmingham Archives and Heritage, Birmingham Central Library).

6   SSB (Sarah Sophia Banks) Papers 20 June 1817 British Museum.

7   Sarah Sophia Banks was the sister of Sir Joseph Banks, a colleague of Boulton's since 1772. Banks had been helpful in obtaining the regal coinage contract (see also entry 21: Otaheite medal). SSB Papers 20 June 1817 British Museum.

Description

Obverse: Bust of Matthew Boulton facing right MATTHAEVS BOULTON No buttons on jacket; below bust PIDGEON F.

Reverse: INVENTAS/ AVT QVI VITAM/ EXCOLVERE PER/ ARTIS (those who have enriched life through discovering arts) in open laurel wreath with single branched stem.

Edge: PATRIS AMICIS M.R.B. (Beloved father of Matthew Robinson Boulton) CIƆIƆCCCXVIIII or plain.

2. JOHN WALKER, *SOHO, STAFFORDSHIRE*, copper-plate etching, 180mm x 241mm, 1798 (private collection)

Walker's etching, depicting the Soho manufactory, was first published in the *Copper-Plate Magazine* in 1798. The image was republished in *The Itinerant* in 1799. The manufactory's Principal Building is shown in the centre of the print's composition with the workshops of Rolling Mill Row to the right and the Mill Pool in front. The Latchet Works are on the left with the buildings of the Mint beyond.[8]

The Principal Building was erected at great expense in the 1760s and served as an imposing architectural symbol of the scale of Boulton's enterprises and the quality

John Walker, SOHO, Staffordshire, *copper plate etching, 180mm x 241mm, 1798.*

---

8   The buildings of the Latchet Works were not completed as shown until 1825-6, what is shown in this image is an intended rather than an actual building.

of their diverse outputs. Boulton had been using prints of the Principal Building to promote his manufactory for some time. But, in the 1790s, he began to facilitate wider circulation of such images to the radical readership of the *Monthly Magazine*, the audience for Stebbing Shaw's *History of Staffordshire*, and the purchasers of the *Copper-Plate Magazine*. Each publication had a particular readership and published a new copper-plate print, but each of these distinct images of the manufactory showed the site from a very similar angle, focusing attention on the Principal Building. However, depending on the anticipated interests of the publications' readerships, different aspects of Boulton's businesses were emphasised in written descriptions of the manufactory that accompanied the prints. The text that was published to accompany Walker's etching for the *Copper-Plate Magazine* was unusually short because that magazine's focus was very much on the images it contained.

PRODUCING THE GOODS AT THE SOHO MINT

3. 1805 BOULTON'S TRAFALGAR MEDAL DIE

Dies were made of specially selected steel and shaped to fit the coining press. They had to withstand high impacts when the die was struck onto the blank discs of copper that would become coins, medals, or tokens. The two examples of dies shown in the Barber Institute exhibition were used to produce medals at Soho. The first die was for a medal to celebrate Nelson's Victory at the Battle of the Nile, and the second was used to strike the famous 1805 Trafalgar medal. The Trafalgar die is incuse (i.e. shows a indented mirror image of Nelson's portrait), and was engraved by Conrad Heinrich Küchler who worked for Boulton from 1793 until his death in 1810 (see catalogue entry 12 for details of the medal).

1805 Trafalgar Medal die Assay Office die 2050A. Base 68mm; top 39-46mm; height 56mm; steel.

Boulton was very particular about the type of steel used to produce dies and he researched the subject thoroughly. Master dies were used to form working dies, which needed to be changed every few hours during extensive minting because they would become worn, resulting in poor quality coins, or tokens. Once used, dies would be destroyed to prevent counterfeiting. Boulton introduced techniques for multiplying dies precisely, and used slightly concave dies which helped to preserve the incuse image.

4. 1788 DROZ COLLAR

Prior to the establishment of the Soho Mint, most coins produced were struck by hand presses and tended to be uneven and misshaped. The Droz collar acted as a third die that worked in addition to those stamping text and imagery on the obverse and reverse sides of a coin or token. It was designed by Jean-Pierre Droz, a French engraver employed by Boulton. The collar was used to enclose the blanks so that the two faces and the edge of the piece were all struck with the same blow of the coining press, either with a plain edge, or one with an inscription. However, the Droz collar proved unsuccessful, and was modified by James Lawson in 1790, resulting in a successful single piece collar that worked with an automatic layer-in that delivered blanks to, and removed coins, medals or tokens from, the press. With the use of collars, each coin became 'perfectly round, and of equal diameter; which is not the case with any other national money ever put in circulation'.[9]

The Royal Mint was not able to introduce collars successfully. Boulton wrote in 1789:

1788 Droz collar Assay Office, total diameter 165mm; central hole 32mm diameter, and 16mm thick; steel.

---

9   Stebbing Shaw, *History of Staffordshire Vol II, 1801*, p.118.

I have also heard of an attempt to strike crown pieces at the Tower in collers [sic], but it was found so troublesome and the coller so hazardous that I believe there never was half a dozen of them struck, and if such a thing had been proposed to the moneyers they would have concluded that it would be worth a peny [sic] at least to make a half peny'.[10]

Description

The Droz collar has six adjustment screws, and a central area made of six parts which have the incuse inscription: RENDER| TO CESAR| THE THIN| GS WHICH| ARE CE| SARS (with three ornamental flowers).

5. 1803 (DATED 1798) BOULTON'S MEDALLIC SCALE Medal (BHM 462)

Boulton's Medallic Scale medal proclaims his invention of the steam powered coining press. Each marked ring indicates the size of a blank coin and the number that could be struck in one minute.[11] It was engraved in French for Matthew Boulton in 1802,[12] in response to a pattern medal in Spanish produced by Jean-Pierre Droz at the Paris Mint, who claimed the invention of the method for making multiple dies in 1801. Thus, a multilingual argument was carried out in three languages on medals! At the time Boulton was investigating the possibility of coining for the French government, during the brief Peace of Amiens, and Droz was hoping to obtain a contract in Spain

1803 '1798' Boulton's Medallic Scale (BHM462) Assay Office 40. 43mm; 30.40g; white metal. Engraver: Dumarest (reverse); Possibly Küchler (obverse).

---

10   MS 3782-21-1, 10 September 1789 MB (Buxton) to Joseph Banks (Soho Square, London).

11   Boulton wrote various versions of the inscription. MS 3782-13-120 Folder 6.

12   The medal reverse was probably engraved in France by Rambert Dumarest who had worked at the Soho Mint.

for the Paris Mint. Droz had worked for Boulton from 1787, and but had been dismissed by July 1791. To add insult to injury, Droz also requested Boulton to send him some steel for medal dies. Boulton called Droz 'the most ungrateful, most ungenerous and basest man I ever had any concern with'.[13]

Description

Obverse: Bust of Matthew Boulton facing right, draped, hair in queue, coat with three buttons. On a wide border around: MATT.BOULTON ESQ[R.] F.R.S. L[N].& ED. F.R. I. &.A.S. (incuse).

Reverse: Legend in French arranged in concentric circles; the outermost on a raised border incuse, the rest relief. M: BOULTON ERIGEA A SOHO ANGL: 1788 UNE MACH: A VAPEUR PR: FRAP: MONN: (400)/1798. IL ER: UNE BIEN SUPERIEURE A 8. BALANCIERS NOVEAUX. (480)/ CES CERC: & CHIF: MARQ: LE DIAM: & NO: DE PIECES FRAP: P: MIN: (560)/P: 8 ENFANS SANS FATIG: DU PL: PET: OU PL: GR: VOLUME(640)/OU DE 8 DIFF: GRAND: ENSEMBLE. ON PEUT (720)/AUGM: L'EFF: AU DEG: NECESSE. (800)

In the centre, head of Science, radiate rays around with (920) above.

Translation

Matthew Boulton erected at Soho, England in 1788, a steam powered machine to strike coins (400). In 1798 he set up a much better one with eight new presses (480) These circles and numbers indicate the diameter and number of pieces struck per minute (560) by eight children without fatigue, of the smallest or greatest volume (640), or of 8 different combinations. One can (720) increase efficiency to the necessary degree (800) (920).

MINTING FOR BRITAIN: TOKENS AND MEDALS

6. 1791 CORNWALL HALFPENNY (D&H Cornwall 2)

Matthew Boulton was heavily involved in the Cornish copper mining industry from 1777 until the 1790s, installing steam engines and taking shares in several mines. He had been trying to bring about an agreement between Thomas Williams of the Anglesey copper mining company, and the Cornish mine owners, to reduce the output of copper in the late-1780s because it was flooding the market and was greatly jeopardising the profits of mines. One of the reasons that Boulton and others were seeking a regal coinage contract was to use up some of the overproduction of

---

13   MS 3782-13-36 Item 48, 30 August 1790 Matthew Boulton (London) to Matthew Robinson Boulton (Germany).

1791 Cornwall Halfpenny Token (D&H Cornwall 2) Assay Office 110. 29mm; 12.80g; bronzed. Engraver: Dumarest.

copper. At one point John Vivian, who commissioned this token, was talking about a coinage of 3000 tons of copper at £84 per ton.[14] However, only around 1 ton of Cornwall halfpennies was coined. Ironically, by the time Boulton gained the regal coinage contract in 1797 the price of copper had risen considerably.[15]

Description
Obverse: A Druid's head with flowing beard, wearing a cowl, within oak branches crossed and tied. R.D. under truncation.

Reverse: Arms of the Duchy of Cornwall: shield (with fifteen circles arranged five, four, three, two and one) surmounted by a ducal coronet. Legend CORNISH COPPER HALF AN OUNCE 1791.

7. 1789 CRONEBANE HALFPENNY Token (D&H Wicklow, Ireland 21)

Boulton had hoped to obtain a regal coinage contract but, as this did not materialise until 1797, he started to make tokens for a variety of customers, including the Associated Irish Mine Company, run by Roe and Co of Macclesfield. This company was established in 1787 at the Cronebane Copper Mine, six miles beyond Wicklow, Ireland, and produced an annual output of 1000 tons of copper between 1787 and 1797. The Cronebane token was the first token in the world to be produced by a

---

14 MS 3782-12-73 Item 14, 18 April 1787 John Vivian (London) to Matthew Boulton (Soho).

15 For the first regal coinage Boulton paid around £108 per ton for copper, but for the 1799 contract £121 and in 1805 the price had risen to £169. MS 3782-17-4 Coinage License 9 June 1797; MS 3782-17-5 Coinage License 4 November 1799; MS 3782-17-6 License to coin 18 April 1805.

1789 Cronebane Halfpenny Token (D&H 21) Assay Office 129. 29mm; 13.00g; bronzed. Engraver: John Gregory Hancock.

steam-powered coining press. They were not yet struck in a collar, as can be seen by their less than regular edges. As Boulton's team had not yet mastered the mass multiplication of dies, and details were put in by hand, there are many varieties of Cronebane tokens with varying positioning of the crosier and date relative to the legend. By September 1789 over 20 tons of tokens had been shipped to Ireland (1,674,185 coins struck at 36 to the pound).

Description
Obverse: Bust of St. Patrick facing right wearing a cape, with a cowl and a mitre. To the right is a crosier tied with a bow of ribbon. Legend: CRONEBANE HALFPENNY.

Reverse: The date 1789 is separated by the arms of the Associated Irish Mine Company (showing two shovels, three pickaxes and a horn) surmounted by a crest in the form of a windlass. Legend: ASSOCIATED IRISH MINE COMPANY.

Edge: plain or PAYABLE AT CRONBANE LODGE OR IN DUBLIN *X*.

8. ANGLESEY TOKEN (D&H Anglesey 387)
There were several hundred varieties of the Anglesey penny or halfpenny tokens showing a Druids Head issued between 1787 and 1791.[16] They were made for the 'Copper King' Thomas Williams of the Parys Mine Company, Anglesey. The copper mine at Parys Mountain was worked as an open quarry and, at the peak of its operations, 60-80,000 tons of ore were produced there annually. By 1787, Thomas

16 Many of these were forgeries or evasive tokens.

Williams had established virtual control over Cornwall's copper output as well as Anglesey's, and he had his own rolling mills and smelting works. His copper was made into sheets for the Royal Navy, used in wire mills and brass works, or sent for shipment overseas from Liverpool and London.

Williams needed coins to pay his thousands of workers. The Parys Mine Company's penny pieces were the first copper tokens issued in Britain in the late-eighteenth century, and also the most numerous. They became very popular due to the lack of regal coinage and, within weeks of their first issue, were being used in London. They were originally produced at Holywell, but a mint was soon set up in Birmingham to manufacture around 250 tons of penny pieces and then 50 tons of halfpenny pieces (13 million coins over four years).

Boulton struck some Anglesey halfpennies dated 1788 in 1789, and more in 1790 and 1791, and pennies in 1792 using previously cut blanks. The issue of 1791 was the first to use Lawson's recently invented collar (see catalogue entry 4), and 16 tons were dispatched by September 1791. The dies for the Anglesey token were engraved by John Gregory Hancock as an outworker. Boulton's Anglesey tokens can be distinguished from those produced by the Parys Mine Company as the letters on the edge inscriptions are larger and more sharply cut.

Description

Obverse: Bust of Druids Head facing left. Twenty two acorns in wreath twelve to left and ten to right in original 1787 version.

Reverse: Cipher PMCo entwined 1787 above. Legend: WE PROMISE TO PAY THE BEARER ONE PENNY. The legend was altered in the later versions to THE ANGLESEY MINES HALFPENNY with various dates to 1791.

1791 Anglesey Halfpenny Token (D&H 387) Assay Office 123. 29mm; 13.25g; bronzed. Engraver: John Gregory Hancock.

Edge: ON DEMAND IN LONDON LIVERPOOL OR ANGLESEY *X* or PAYABLE IN ANGLESEY LONDON OR LIVERPOOL *X* or on Boulton halfpenny PAYABLE IN ANGLESEY OR LONDON < < < < < < < <.

9. 1796 (dated 1794) PENRYN VOLUNTEERS HALFPENNY (D&H Cornwall 4)

The importance of artistic merit in engraving can be seen in the beautiful and complex design of the Penryn Halfpenny tokens ordered by Sir George Chapman George and dedicated to Sir Francis Bassett (1757-1835). The Bassett family had been living in Cornwall for 700 years and had considerable interests in the Cornish copper mines. Sir Francis, an old acquaintance of Boulton, was appointed in 1785 as Chairman of the Cornish Copper Company. The company smelted and sold Cornish copper ores. However Bassett opposed some of Boulton's plans to regulate the mining industry and prevent overproduction.

Bassett, the commander of the Penryn Volunteers, was ennobled, in reward for raising a force of miners to defend Falmouth from Spanish and French fleets in 1794. He also erected a battery of four twelve pounder cannons at Portreath Bay on the north Cornish coast as a defence against privateers. Bassett became Baron de Dunstanville in June 1796 and the tokens that were produced for him at Soho were dispatched in September 1796.

Description

Obverse: The arms of Penryn: a shield decorated with dots, showing laureated bust of bearded man facing left, and surmounted by a plumed helmet. Surrounded by military trophies, including a drum, flags, swords and pikes. Legend on a tasselled riband: PENRYN VOLUNTEERS.

1796 (dated 1794) Penryn Volunteers Halfpenny (D&H 4) Assay Office 112. 28.5mm; 10.50g; copper. Engraver: Küchler or Ponthon.

In exergue: FIRST INROLLED APRIL 3. 1794.

Reverse: The arms of Lord de Dunstanville, surmounted by a baronet's coronet, with a unicorn on either side. Motto on a scroll above the crest: PRO REGE ET POPULO (for the king and people).

In exergue: LORD DE DUNSTANVILLE COLONEL.

10. 1802 LOYAL BIRMINGHAM LIGHT HORSE VOLUNTEERS MEDAL

For most of the time that Matthew Boulton ran the Soho Mint, Britain was at war. The Loyal Birmingham Volunteers was established in 1802, as a successor to the Birmingham Loyal Association, set up in 1797, as a response to a threatened invasion by the French. The 1797 Battalion had one company of foot, and one of 500 men on horseback. A medal, possibly produced at Soho, was presented at a review held on 4 June 1798 on Birmingham Heath near Soho to celebrate the occasion. Matthew Boulton's son, Matthew Robinson Boulton (1770-1842) was an officer in the 1st Battalion, Loyal Birmingham Volunteers, who escorted Lord Nelson when he visited Birmingham in 1802. It would be interesting to follow up the history of the individuals named on the inscriptions of the medals. Who were Job Hunt and Lieutenant John Porter?

Description

Obverse: Allegory of Peace facing left presents a medal to a soldier in Roman dress (Mars) facing right. Pedestal entwined with laurel in middle. Pile of items to right of Peace which includes bust, pallet and potter's wheel. Building to left, possibly St Phillips, Birmingham. Legend FOR TRUE PATRIOTISM.

In exergue: PEACE MDCCCII.

1802 Birmingham Loyal Association Assay Office 235. 48mm; 47.30g; silver. Engraver: Hancock.

Reverse: Oak wreath surrounding inscription on oblong block with above PRESENTED TO *name of individual* (in italic script) and below BY THE TOWN/ OF/ BIRMINGHAM/ MAY XXVIII/ MDCCCII (28 May 1802).

Assay Office 233   Job Hunt/ 4th Comp^y/ Birm^m Loy^l Associat^n
Assay Office 235   Lieut^t Jno Porter/ 7th Comp^y/ Birm^m Loy^l Associat^n

11. 1798 BRITISH VICTORIES and 1798 DAVISON'S NILE MEDAL (BHM 458 and BHM 447) (reverses only)

Medals pertaining to recent naval victories were distributed widely, and were made by Birmingham manufacturers such as Westwood and Kempson, as well as at Soho Mint. The British Victories medal by Küchler may have been partly made in advance, as the bust of George III was started in 1795, but it was not struck until 1800. It commemorated the victories won by Britain during the year 1798. These included Nelson's victory over the French fleet at the Battle of the Nile and the capture of Minorca. Bonaparte had attacked Egypt in July 1798. On 1 August, a scouting vessel from Nelson's fleet found the French fleet anchored close to shallow water in Aboukir Bay to the south of Alexandria, Egypt. The resulting battle lasted all night and the victory gave the British complete control of the Mediterranean.

Another medal, commissioned by Alexander Davidson, Nelson's prize agent, was given to everyone who served in the Nile battle. The reverse shows the fleet arranged for attack before the battle, and the inscription gives the opening of Nelson's dispatch to George III. The bill, dated 15 May 1801, shows a cost of £112 14s for engraving and completion of 25 gold, 154 silver, 506 gilt and 6,530 tin medals, with the cost of the gold and silver being £334 6s.[17]

Description (Victories)

Obverse: Bust of George III facing left, wearing a dress wig with hair in tight, neat rolls. Elaborate uniform with large medallion. Legend: GEORGIUS III. D: G. M. BR. FR. ET H. REX.

Signed in field below bust: C.H. KÜCHLER. FEC. on truncation.

Reverse: Britannia, with spear and shield, seated on a trophy pile of arms. This includes cannon, anchor, spar with sails, flags, pike, etc. Held up in her hand is a figure of Victory. Legend: MARI VICTRIX. TERRAQUE INVICTA (Victorious at sea, unvanquished on land).

In exergue: AVITUM TRANSCENDIT/ HONOREM/ MDCCXCVIII (Surpasses forefather's renown *1798*) Signed above exergual line: C H K.

---

17   MS 3782-6-195 Item 50 Bill dated 15 May 1801 to Alexander Davison.

Left: 1798 British Victories (BHM 458) Assay 23. 48mm; 38.65g; bronzed. Engraver: Küchler.
Right: 1798 Battle of the Nile (BHM 447) Assay 21. 48mm; 38.65g; bronzed. Engraver: Küchler.

Description (Nile)
Obverse: Allegory of peace standing on the left on a rock, holding an olive spray in extended right hand, and leaning on an oval medallion/shield bearing a profile bust of Nelson and inscription EUROPE'S HOPE AND BRITAIN'S GLORY. Behind open sea. Around REAR-ADMIRAL LORD NELSON OF THE NILE Signed on rock: C.H.K.

    Reverse: ALMIGHTY GOD HAS BLESSED HIS MAJESTY'S ARMS. Scene of naval battle in Aboukir Bay, the French at anchor, the English fleet going into action.

    In exergue: VICTORY OF THE NILE/AUGUST 1. 1798.

    Signed on exergual line: M.B. SOHO C.H. KÜCHLER. FEC.

    Edge: Incuse legend FROM ALEX^R. DAVIDSON, ESQ^R. ST. JAMES' SQUARE = A TRIBUTE OF REGARD.

12. 1805 BOULTON'S TRAFALGAR MEDAL (BHM 584) (see catalogue entry 3)
Many articles have been written on the Trafalgar medal as well as the monograph written by Sir Nicholas Goodison in 2007.[18] It is probably the best known of Boulton's medals and was produced at his own expense for presentation to the marines and seamen who took part in the action off Cape Trafalgar on 21 October 1805. The battle lasted around seven hours. Seventeen enemy ships were captured, one was burnt and the others fled. Nelson died as a result of a musket ball wound received early in the engagement. His body was buried in the crypt in St. Paul's cathedral on 9 January 1806.

18   Nicholas Goodison, *Matthew Boulton's Trafalgar Medal*, Birmingham, 2007.

1805 Trafalgar Medal (BHM 584) Assay Office 45. 48mm; 55.70g; silver. Engraver: Küchler.

19,000 medals were made in tin and copper with some silver and gold medals produced for presentation at court. Great care was taken to get a lifelike portrait of Nelson. Boulton was helped in this by his friend J. F. Tuffin. The first die was based on a sketch by Lady Beechey, from the portrait by her husband, Sir William Beechey, painted in 1801, but was not approved by Nelson's family. A second attempt from a miniature owned by Lady Hamilton and a drawing by de Koster (da Costa) was also not accepted, and the final version was engraved by Küchler from a wax image by Catherine Andras, modelled from life in 1805.

Description

Obverse: HORATIO VISCOUNT NELSON. K.B. DUKE OF BRONTE. &c. Uniformed bust of Nelson facing left. Signed on truncation: C.H.K.

Reverse: on a ribbon above ENGLAND EXPECTS EVERY MAN WILL DO HIS DUTY. Panoramic view of the battle of Trafalgar. 15 sailing ships in smoke of battle.

In exergue: TRAFALGAR OCT^R 21.1805 Signed on exergual line: K.

Edge: Inscribed TO THE HEROES OF TRAFALGAR FROM M:BOULTON or plain.

13. 1794 LANCASTER/ECCLESTON HALFPENNY TOKEN (D&H Lancashire 57)

The image on this token shows three important aspects of the eighteenth-century British economy – agriculture, manufacturing, and commerce – symbolised by a plough, a flying shuttle, and a ship's rigging. The token was struck in the style of the later regal copper coinage of 1797 with a broad raised rim. Just over a ton of Lancaster tokens were produced and were sent to Liverpool by Worthing & Gilbert's canal boat in seven casks containing 21 cwt of copper halfpennies. The engraving of

1794 Lancaster/Eccleston Halfpenny Token (D&H 57) Assay Office 116. 28.5mm; 12.80g; copper. Engraver: Ponthon.

the dies cost 5 guineas, the coining expenses were £44 10s 6d and the total cost of £57 2s 6d for 109,247 copper tokens.[19]

Daniel Eccleston was a coin collector, who had spent several years in Antigua and Barbados, and finally settled in Lancaster and worked as a liquor merchant and insurance broker. His obituary appeared in the Lancaster Gazette in 1816, but Eccleston wrote responding to it the following week, and was still writing to the Soho Mint in 1820!

Description:
Obverse: Bust of Daniel Eccleston facing left. Legend incuse on a raised rim: DANIEL ECCLESTON LANCASTER. Ponthon on truncation of the left shoulder.

Reverse: Symbols of industry and agriculture: a plough and a flying shuttle in the foreground, with the masts and rigging of a ship behind, her lower sails furled and apparently lying at a wharf. Beyond the ship is a bay with a hill at the extreme left. Legend incuse on a raised rim: THE LANCASHIRE HALFPENNY 1794.

In exergue: AGRICULT. MANUFACT. & COMMERCE.

Edge: PAYABLE. IN. LANCASTER LIVERPOOL. &. MANCHESTER.

14. ANON. *DESIGN FOR A BOARD OF AGRICULTURE MEDAL*, ink and wash on paper, 1793 (Eimer 853)

Agricultural medals were given by various local societies for skill in ploughing, rearing of prize cattle, etc. The issuing of such awards can be seen as relating to a growing emphasis on meritocracy in various areas of British life. This design was

19   MS 3782-3-13 Mint Day Book 1791-1795.

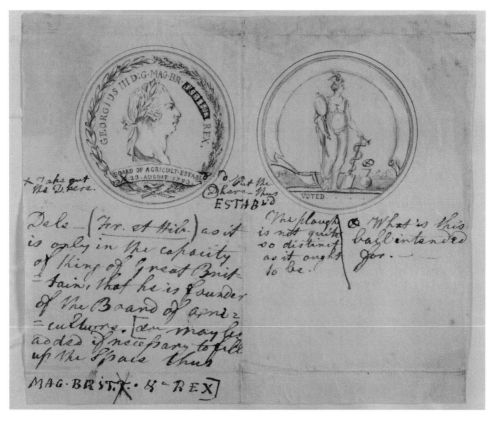

Designs in Timmins Album Timmins Volume 1 Reference 82934 Item 34 (approx 100mm x 60mm) (Reproduced courtesy of Birmingham Archives and Heritage).

produced for the Board of Agriculture, an organisation with which Boulton corresponded on various matters, including the powering of grain mills using steam engines.[20]

The design for the medal which is displayed in the exhibition includes written corrections to the first version of the inscription. The engraver [Küchler] was told to delete the FR ET HIB which is usual in the title of the monarch, 'as it is only in the capacity of King of Great Britain, that he is founder of the Board of Agriculture'.[21] Versions of the resulting medal were awarded until 1803.

---

20   The Albion Mill in London was set up in 1784, and was functional from 1786. Unfortunately it burnt down in 1791. H. W. Dickinson, *Matthew Boulton*, Cambridge, 1937, p.123.

21   Birmingham Archives Boulton & Watt Pt 1 Timmins collection Reference 82934 Board of Agriculture designs.

Description

Obverse: GEORGIUS III. D:G. MAG. BR. REX (George III, by the grace of God, King of Great Britain).

Laureate head of King facing right with the whole in wreath of laurel and corn. In scroll underneath head: BOARD OF AGRICULTURE ESTABL^D. 23.AUG.1793.

Signed on truncation: C.H.K.

Reverse: Female figure standing facing right holding in left hand a spade with a snake twined round handle and in right hand she holds a mirror, Other agricultural instruments and a plough are in the foreground. In the background landscape with field and cottage. Above is a blank ribbon label for inscription.

In exergue: VOTED (space for date).

Signed on exergual line: C.H. KÜCHLER. FEC:

15. 1795 (DATED 1797) MARRIAGE OF PRINCE OF WALES (BHM 392)

The Prince of Wales was married to Princess Caroline of Brunswick on 8 April 1795, but the medal is dated 1797 by mistake, and was not issued at the time. The example shown in the exhibition was owned by Sarah Sophia Banks, the sister of Sir Joseph Banks, President of the Royal Society, and Matthew Boulton's friend. She was an avid collector of coins, medals and tokens. By 1807 Matthew Boulton had arranged for her to be sent specimens of every item struck at the Soho Mint. On 18 May 1807 John Phillp wrote that he had

the satisfaction of sending the medal of the Prince & Princess of Wales struck for Frogmore Fete, which Mr Boulton permitted me to take out of his Cabinet, on my mentioning your desire to possess one. The Die for the reverse being

1795 (dated 1797) Marriage of Prince of Wales (BHM 392) Assay Office 17. 48mm; 50.25g; bronzed. Engraver: Küchler.

destroyed, this is the only Medal remaining at Soho. [...] Mr Boulton has given me permission to send, and also to reserve for your valuable collection an impression from every new Coin that may hereafter to be struck at Soho.[22]

Sarah Sophia Banks also collected cuttings from newspapers showing advertisements for various medals.

Description
Obverse: Conjoined busts of the Prince of Wales and Princess Caroline, facing right. Caroline is wearing a large feather on her hat. George is bareheaded with long hair caught back. Lace collar, large buckle/button on coat. Legend: GEORG. WALL. PRINC. ET CAROLIN. BRUNS. PR. with C.H. KÜCHLER under busts.

F. Reverse: Winged figure of Hymen, the god of marriage, standing facing right holding a flaming torch in left hand and in right hand the shield of Great Britain and Brunswick-Wolfenbuttel. In background extensive view of London showing St. Paul's cathedral. JUNXIT HYMEN TAEDIS ILLUSTRIBUS AMBOS (Hymen has joined them both in illustrious marriage).

In exergue: NUPTIAE REGIAE LOND. / MDCCXCVII (Royal marriage in London 1797). Signed on exergual line: C.H. KÜCHLER. FEC:

MINTING FOR BRITAIN: REGAL COINAGE

16. PATTERN HALFPENNIES
There are seventeen versions of Droz pattern halfpennies with varying details such as the number of leaves and berries on the wreath, the formation of the hair curls, or the position of the spear, arms and legs.[23] In one pattern version Britannia is nude. Jean-Pierre Droz had been employed in 1787 to engrave a portrait die of George III, which was needed for the expected regal coinage contract. Some versions are signed Droz F (incuse), and the date may also be 1788 or 1790. Droz proved to be very unsatisfactory and left the Soho Mint in 1791. Further pattern halfpenny coins were struck in 1795 with the reverse Britannia from the old 1790 Droz halfpenny punch, and the obverse die of George III produced for the 1791 guinea by Thomas Wyon. But the broad raised rim spoilt the overall appearance of the design, and had to be narrowed at the base to allow space to include the date.

---

22   Sarah Sophia Banks album British Museum.
23   These are described fully in Peck, *Copper Coins*.

1788 Pattern Halfpenny Proof Late Soho (Peck 965) Assay Office 78. 31mm; 15.90g; bronzed gilt. Engraver: Droz.

Description
Obverse: Bust of George III facing right. Legend: GEORGIUS III D:G. REX with diamond stops. Some with D.F. on truncation.

Reverse: Britannia seated facing left BRITANNIA.1788.

In exergue: Ship's rudder and palm branch crossed.

Edge: RENDER| TO CESAR| THE THIN| GS WHICH| ARE CE| SARS three ornaments.

17. 1797 and 1799 COINAGE

The regal coinage contract that had led Boulton to commission pattern coins from Droz did not materialise for several years. In the meantime, Boulton had perfected his Mint machinery by making money for a variety of customers at home and abroad. After waiting more than a decade, in 1797 Boulton finally won the regal contract to strike 480 tons of one penny pieces at 32/lb, with 20 tons of two pence at 16/lb to follow. Copper was obtained, the designs agreed, and coining commenced on 19 June 1797. The first delivery of pence reached Charlotte Matthews, Boulton's agent in London, on 26 July. By January 1798 2,500 casks of coins had been distributed as far as Newfoundland, the Cape Colony (South Africa) and Australia, with a final total of 43,969,204 pennies and 722,180 two pence minted. The 1797 copper coinage was the first issue of copper pennies in Britain since Anglo-Saxon times. They became known as 'cartwheel pennies' due to their broad rim which was to protect the engraving from wear in use.

The cartwheel pennies were readily accepted by the general public but, the twopences (weighing 2oz; 56.70g) were found to be too heavy. Not only were they difficult to use, they also were very difficult to make. So, Matthew Boulton decided to reconstruct his mint, incorporating technical improvements in a new mint that was more efficient and quieter. For the 1799 coinage of halfpennies and farthings the cartwheel rim was replaced by a smaller raised rim with beaded border, and had slightly curved fields. The blanks were milled with oblique markings on the edges to make counterfeiting more difficult. The portrait of George III and the Britannia image were retained on currency issues (but George III appears with a crown on 1799 pattern halfpennies).

Boulton had started striking halfpence by May 1799, and had 20 tons prepared by August but did not have any written instructions to proceed until 4 November 1799. This order was for 550 tons of copper with 10 halfpennies to every farthing (36/lb and 72/lb respectively; a reduced weight due to increased prices in copper). Production ceased by July 1800 when 3,540 casks of halfpence and 176 casks of farthings had been sent; an amazing total of 42,480,000 halfpennies and 4,224,000 farthings.

Description

Obverse: Draped and laureated bust of George III facing right. Legend: incuse on a broad raised rim GEORGIUS. III. D:G. REX.

Reverse: Britannia in long clinging drapery seated facing left on a rock amidst waves. In her right hand she holds an olive branch. Her left hand, held down, clasps a trident. By her left side is an oval shield, bearing the combined crosses of St. George and St. Andrew, heraldically coloured. On the rock to the right are three dots raised and below the shield SOHO. In the distance on the sea is a 3-masted warship. All within a broad raised rim bearing the legend (incuse) BRITANNIA above and 1797 below.

1797 Cartwheel Two Pence (Peck 1068) Assay Office 68. 42mm; 56.70g; bronzed. Engraver: Küchler.

18. 1804 BANK OF ENGLAND REGENERATED FIVE SHILLING DOLLAR TOKEN

The number of silver coins issued by the Royal Mint was very small for the first 55 years of George III's reign (1760-1820). Many were worn and easily counterfeited, and pieces of eight (from the Spanish eight *reales*) circulated freely in Britain. In 1797 some of these Spanish coins were overstamped by an oval punch showing George III's head. In 1804 the punch was changed to an octagonal shape. However, silver coins continued to be easily counterfeited and the overstruck coins were withdrawn. In 1804 Boulton suggested that his Soho Mint could completely overstrike the image because it was easier to strike the already alloyed, rolled and blanked Spanish coins than to start from scratch. He proceeded to prepare several dies, and from 28 April the Spanish coins left the Bank of England for Soho Mint. By 27 June 1804, 1,005,523 dollars had been overstruck, or 'regenerated' as Boulton preferred to say, plus 1,420 proof pieces struck from new silver. The order was repeated until, by April 1811, a total of 4.5 million tokens were made, all dated 1804. A similar scheme for the Bank of Ireland was agreed with the tokens valued at six shillings rather than five.

Description

Obverse: Laureated bust of George III in profile facing right with long flowing hair in ringlets, reaching to the shoulders which are draped. C.H.K. on truncation. Legend: GEORGIUS III DEI GRATIA REX.

Reverse: Britannia seated facing left with spear in left hand and laurel spray in right hand; cornucopia beneath shield with oval shield, bearing the combined crosses of St. George, St. Patrick and St. Andrew, all within oval band inscribed FIVE

1804 Bank of England Regenerated Token Assay Office 66. 40mm; 26.90g; silver. Engraver: Küchler.

SHILLING DOLLAR with mural crown above. Legend: BANK OF ENGLAND 1804 within raised grained rim.

19. 1801 UNION OF BRITAIN AND IRELAND (BHM 523 and BHM 534)

The Act of Union between Britain and Ireland became law on 1 January 1801. There had been serious insurrection in Ireland in 1797 and 1798, and such uprisings were particularly worrying for the government in London during the French revolutionary wars. It was claimed that a union would benefit both countries' trade and commerce. A contemporary advertisement gives a full description of the medal:

> Two crowned Female Figures, representing BRITANNIA and HIBERNIA united by their Right Hands in Friendship and Interest. Britannia holds in her Left Hand the Caduceus of Mercury which rests of the Arms of Great Britain, to shew that the [sic] will ever support the Trade and Commerce of the United Kingdoms. Hibernia supports with her Left Hand the Arms of Ireland, behind which is the Cornucopia, distributing, by Means of the Union, Riches and Plenty. She also holds an Olive Branch, as an Emblem of Peace and Sincerity. On the Sea are seen two ships, British and Irish, sailing in Company, to shew that the Blessings of Trade and Commerce are divided between the two Nations JUNGUNTUR OPES, FIRMATUR IMPERIUM [their wealth or resources are united, and the Empire is confirmed or consolidated][24]

1801 Union of Britain and Ireland (BHM 524) Assay Office 32. 48mm; 53.90g; gilt. Engraver: Küchler.

---

24   Sarah Sophia Banks album, British Museum.

Description (BHM 523)

Obverse: Draped bust of George III with simple brooch on shoulder with hair in queue. Signed in field below bust: C.H.K. Three dots on truncation. Legend: GEORGIUS III. D:G. BRITANNIARUM REX. FIDEI. DEF. &c. Signed in field below bust: C.H.K. Three dots on truncation.

Reverse: JUNGUNTUR OPES FIRMATUR IMPERIUM (wealth united, Empire consolidated) Britannia standing, shaking hands with Hibernia, seascape background. Shield with British flag and shield with harp.

In exergue: 1.JAN/MDCCCI with ornament underneath. Signed on exergual line: C.H. KÜCHLER. F.C.

20. 1805 AND 1806 IRISH and BRITISH COINAGE

The problem of a lack of small change was worse in Ireland than in Britain. So, in 1805 and 1806 Boulton minted the official coinage for Ireland using the 1799 obverse design of George III from the British coinage and a harp design on the reverse. Penny pieces were struck at 26/lb, shipped by canal to Liverpool and then carried to Dublin under military escort; the first delivery arriving there in June 1805. Halfpennies followed on 9 July and the final cargo of these left on 24 February 1806. The single batch of farthings dated 1806 were sent at the same time. In total 8,788,416 pence, 49,795,200 halfpence and 4,996,992 farthings to Ireland (over 63 million coins). The 1806-1807 British regal coinage of pennies, halfpennies and farthings followed, but with slightly increased sized coins. The portrait of George III was altered to show him with short hair, but the image of Britannia remained the same. The reverses showed the individual emblems of Britain and Ireland: the harp and Britannia. In this third regal coinage over 165 million coins were made at the Soho Mint, providing a national iconography accessible to everyone in Britain.

Left and centre: 1805 Irish Penny (Dowle and Finn 593) Assay Office 102. 33mm gilt; 17.45g. Right: 1806 British Penny (Peck 1321) Assay Office 74. 34mm gilt; 18.85g.

Description (Irish)

Obverse: Laureated, draped bust of George III in profile with long hair. K. on truncation. Legend: GEORGIUS III D:G. REX. Raised rim and beaded border.

Reverse: Irish harp surmounted by crown. HIBERNIA with below 1805.

Edge: centre grained.

Description (British)

Obverse: Draped bust of George III facing right with short hair. Legend: GEORGIUS III D:G. REX 1806 Raised rim with beaded border.

Reverse: Britannia seated facing left BRITANNIA.

Edge: centre grained.

MINTING FOR THE WIDER WORLD

21. 1772 'OTAHEITE' MEDAL also known as CAPTAIN COOK'S SECOND VOYAGE TO THE PACIFIC MEDAL or RESOLUTION AND ADVENTURE MEDAL (BHM 165)

The eighteenth century was a period of global exploration and expansion of British rule. The first medal made by Boulton was for Captain Cook's second voyage to the Pacific in July 1772. Cook's ship, *Resolution*, sailed with 110 men, and Captain Tobias Furneaux, in *Adventure*, with 80. Cook took goods intended for presentation to natives: eight casks of nails, a cask of edge tools, and two casks of glass, (including green glass earrings), all supplied by Boulton and Fothergill.[25] Sir Joseph Banks, who had been

1772 Otaheite Medal (BHM165) Assay Office 2. 42mm; 33.45g; brass with loop. Engraver J. Westwood.

---

25 http://www2.sl.nsw.gov.au/banks/series. Series 6, Image CY 3003 109 (accessed Nov 2008).

on the first expedition in 1768 when he was 25 years old, commissioned 2000 platina (brass) medals for the voyage but decided in May 1772 to withdraw from the expedition. A new die was made by Boulton for 100 silver medals, costing £57 12s 3d, given to Banks' friends. Thus, there are subtle differences in the surviving medals; the brass example, as shown in the exhibition, has a vertical anchor and the silver version's anchor is horizontal.

Description

Obverse: Laureate bust of George III facing right. B.F. on truncation. Double rim. GEORGE. III. KING. OF. GR. BRITAIN. FRANCE. AND. IRELAND. ETC.

Reverse: Two frigates viewed from astern. Anchor vertical or horizontal. RESOLUTION ADVENTURE.

In exergue: SAILED. FROM. ENGLAND / MARCH MDCCLXXII.

Edge: slightly rounded.

22 and 23. 1793 EXECUTION MEDALS OF LOUIS XVI OF FRANCE AND MARIE ANTOINETTE

In 1789, opinion in Britain had been favourable towards the French Revolution. However, the abolition of the French monarchy in September 1792, followed by Louis XVI, and then Marie Antoinette's, trial and guillotining, caused considerable concern in Britain. The Soho Mint produced medals that appealed to British people who were revolted by regicide. One of the designs elicited viewers' sympathy for the ex-monarch by depicting him saying his final farewell to his family. Boulton had intended to issue such a medal before Conrad Heinrich Küchler came to work for

Left: 1793 Louis XVI Execution Farewell Assay Office 4 (obverse). 48mm; 46.50g; bronzed. Centre: 1793 Louis XVI Execution Farewell Assay Office 5 (reverse). 48mm; 54.00g; bronzed Engraver: Küchler. Right: 1793 Execution of Louis XVI of France (Death) (reverse) Assay Office 6. 51mm 60.70g; bronzed. Engraver: Küchler and Ponthon.

1793 Execution of Marie Antoinette Assay Office 10. 48mm; 54.50g; bronzed. Engraver: Küchler.

him, and had the reverse engraved by Noel-Alexandre Ponthon. Another medal portrays Louis' execution and a third the execution of Marie Antoinette, representing her as a mother torn away from her children to face a horrific death.[26]

Description (Louis XVI and Marie-Antoinette Farewell)
Obverse: Conjoined bust of Louis XVI and Marie Antoinette facing right. LUD. XVI D: G. FR. ET NAV. REX. MAR. ANT. AVSTR. REG. C.H.K. on truncation.

Below: FATI INIQI (of an unjust fate).

Reverse: AN EST DOLOR PAR DOLORI NOSTRO (Is there a grief equal to our grief?) Four figures grouped with two adults and two children. Female figure to rear facing right. Drapery behind and window overlooking public square. Hat to left on floor.

In exergue: NATUS XXIII AUG. MDCCLIV. / SUCC. X. MAY MDCCLXXIV. / DECOLL. XXI JAN. / MDCCXCIII (born 23.8.1754; acceded to the throne 10.5.1774; beheaded 21.1.1793) On exergual line: C.H. KÜCHLER FEC.

Description (Louis XVI Death)
Obverse: Conjoined bust of Louis XVI and Marie Antoinette facing right. C.H.K. on truncation Legend: LUD. XVI D: G. FR. ET NAV. REX. MAR. ANT. AUSTR. REG. with below: FATI INIQI (of an unjust fate).

Reverse: View of the buildings of Place de la Révolution (previously known as Place Louis XV and now known as Place de la Concorde) with the execution of Louis XVI. Large crowd surrounding guillotine where the executioner is showing the

---

26   David Bindman, *The Shadow of the Guillotine*, British Museum, London, 1989, pp.22-23.

head of Louis XVI to the crowd. Figures of bystanders in foreground and then a row of soldiers with flags flying. Legend: CRINEMQUE ROTANTES SANGUINEUM POPULIS ULULARUNT TRISTIA GALLI (They waved the bloody head to the crowds/people and the French wailed their sad lament).

In exergue: XXI JANUARIUS/ANNO MDCCXCIII (21 January 1793).

Signed on exergual line P.

Description (Marie-Antoinette Death)

Obverse: Bust of Marie Antoinette facing left. MARIA ANTON. AUSTR. FR. ET NAV. REGINA.(Marie Antoinette of Austria, France and Navarre) Below: NAT. 2 NOV. 1755. NUP. 16 MAY 1770. COR. 11 JUN 1775.

Signed on truncation H.K.

Reverse: Queen, Marie Antoinette, being transported to her execution at the guillotine in October 1793. She is in a horse-drawn cart in front of a large crowd. Guillotine in middle. Large crowd with classical buildings.

ALTERA VENIT VICTIMA (A second victim has come).

In exergue: XVI. OCT. MDCCXCIII (16 Oct 1793).

24. SUMATRA (Known as Bencoolen)

One of Matthew Boulton's most important customers at the Soho Mint was the Honourable East India Company (EIC) which traded with the Indian subcontinent and China, mainly in cotton, silk, indigo, tea, saltpetre and opium. Increasingly controlled by the British government, the EIC was frequently involved in hostilities with other countries' trading companies. By 1786 the company functioned as a regularised subsidiary of the Crown.

Left: 1804 Sumatra (4 keping) Assay Office 188 (obverse). 30mm; 12.95g; copper.
Right: 1804 Sumatra (1 keping) Assay Office 190 (reverse). 21mm; 3.25g; copper.

Sumatra is an island in western Indonesia where an English trading centre was established in 1685 at Bencoolen (Bengkulu). It was the 1786 order of 18 tons of copper coins for Sumatra for the EIC that stimulated the idea of the Soho Mint. The order, consisting of nearly 3 million coins, was struck in London on hand presses set up by Soho workers, and was completed in late May 1787.

The original 1786 design for the Sumatra issue of coins consisted of a simple heart-shaped shield, the balemark of the East India Company (as seen below on the Madras coin) with a Persian inscription in the Malay language, giving the value of the coin and the Hegira date (1200).[27] There were repeat orders in 1787 and 1798 that used the same design but,[28] by 1804, the obverse had become a much more elaborate depiction of the EIC coat of arms. The latter design is also found on 1804 coins for Bombay, and 1803 and 1808 coins for Madras. One unifying iconography was now used on coins for most areas under EIC control with differing reverses; a bit like the modern symbol used on the reverse of all euro coins, with the other side bearing a different design for each member state.

Description

Obverse: Heart shaped balemark of the East India Company 1786 under.

By 1804: EAST INDIA COMPANY. In centre arms of East India Company. Inscription in scroll in very small lettering AUSPICIO REGIS & SENATUS ANGLIÆ (Under the auspices of the King and the English Parliament) with 1804 under.

Reverse: Persian inscription giving the value of the coin and the Hegira date [4 *Ampat Keping* (4 keping) 2 *Dua Keping* (2 keping) 1 *Satu Keping* (1 keping) 1٢19 (1804)].

25. INDIA MADRAS PRESIDENCY

Madras was one of the three provinces established by the Honourable East India Company (EIC) as a result of Pitt's India Act in 1785. It covered a large area of southern India, with the capital at Madras (Chennai). The design for the 1794 and 1797 issues of Madras coins featured the EIC balemark but was accompanied by a more complex coat of arms on the other side. The coins also featured a broad raised cartwheel rim, later to be used in the British regal coinage in 1797. The design was struck in denominations of 1/48th and 1/96th part of a rupee (34 and 68 to the pound weight) in order to be integrated into a number of local coinage

---

27 The Hegira/Hejira (or Islamic year) in 1804 was AH 1219 and commenced on 12 April 1804. The Islamic calendar dates from the flight of Muhammad from Mecca to Medina in AD 622.

28 The 1787 order was for 30 tons dated 1787, and consisted of around 12 million coins, and the 1798 order 2.5 million. In 1804 14,447,358 coins were made, giving a grand total of over 28 million coins.

Left and centre: 1794 India Madras (1/48 rupee) (Pridmore 311) Assay Office 163. 30mm; 13.35g; gilt. Right: 1808 India Madras Presidency 20 cash (Pridmore 198) Assay Office 165. 31mm; 9.35g; bronzed.

systems. Most of the EIC orders from the Soho Mint were shipped by canal to Hull, and then to London to be loaded onto the Company vessels bound for India at St. Botolph's Wharf. In total 4,616,129 larger and 9,102,868 smaller Madras rupees were produced in 1794 and another 16,535,202 in 1797. By 1803, the coins for Madras were being made in four values and had a completely different reverse design with a Persian inscription that gave the value of the coin (also written in roman numerals) with the word CASH. The design remained the same in 1808.

Description
Obverse: Legend: AUSPICIO REGIS ET SENATUS ANGLIÆ (Under the auspices of the King and the English Parliament) on a broad raised rim incuse. On the remainder of the broad rim in a sunken panel with letters in relief TO ONE RUPEE.

In centre arms of East India Company; Inscription in very small lettering on ribbon UNITED EAST INDIA CO with 48 or 96 under.

Reverse: Balemark of the East India Company (heart shaped shield quartered with diagonal cross and marked E V I C with extended 4 symbol) within a broad raised rim inscribed (incuse) UNITED EAST INDIA COMPANY 1794 or 1797.

By 1804 the reverse was a Persian inscription giving the value, plus the value in roman numerals and CASH and this design was reused in 1808.

Bīst Kās chahar falūs ast (twenty cash makes four falūs).
In exergue: XX. CASH.
Reverse: Persian inscription *Dah Kās do falūs ast* (ten cash makes two falūs).
In exergue: X CASH.
Reverse: Persian inscription *Panj Kās yek falūs ast* (five cash makes one falūs).

In exergue: V CASH.

Reverse: Persian inscription *Kās* (cash).

In exergue: I CASH.

26. 1792 dated 1791 SIERRA LEONE

The Sierra Leone coinage, the first decimal issue produced in Britain, consisted of less than a million pieces, all dated 1791 but made in 1792, 1793, and 1796 to 1806. They are a complex series of coins, consisting of dollars with the unit 1 or 100, 50 cents, 20 cents, 10 cents and pennies struck as cents, all made originally as a silver currency. Many of the 10 cent pieces sent to Sierra Leone in 1793 were destroyed in a fire on board the *York* shortly after arriving in Africa.

The importance of the Sierra Leone pieces lies not so much in their numbers, but in the fact that they were made for a colony of freed slaves that was established in 1791, fifteen years before the British abolition of the slave trade. The coins entered circulation at a time when millions of slaves were still being transported by British ships across the Atlantic. The symbolism of the white and black hands clasped in friendship is an image that points to growing opposition to slavery.

Description

Obverse: Lion face on Legend: SIERRA LEONE COMPANY.

In exergue: AFRICA.

Reverse: Clasped hands: right hand shaded. Above and below 100 (50; 20; 10; 1). Legend: ONE DOLLAR PIECE 1791 (or HALF DOLLAR PIECE: 20 CENT PIECE; 10 CENT PIECE; ONE PENNY PIECE; ONE CENT PIECE).

The coin design is the same in each case except for the value of the coin.

1792 (dated 1791) Sierra Leone (50 cent) (obverse left, reverse right) Assay Office 178. 31mm; 13.20g; silver.

Bibliography

R. C. Bell, *Commercial Coins 1787-1804*, Corbitt and Hunter, Newcastle, 1963.

R. C. Bell, *Tradesmen's Tickets and Private Tokens 1785-1819*, Corbitt and Hunter, Newcastle, 1966.

R. C. Bell, *Specious Tokens and those struck for GENERAL circulation 1784-1804*, Corbitt and Hunter, Newcastle, 1968.

Stacey Boldrick and Richard Clay (eds.), *Iconoclasm: Contested Objects, Contested Terms*, Ashgate, Aldershot, 2007.

J. Bouchary, *Les Manieurs d'argent à Paris à la fin du XVIIIe siècle*, Paris, 1942.

Witt Bowden, *Industrial society in England towards the end of the eighteenth century*, Macmillan, New York, 1925.

Laurence Brown, *A Catalogue of British Historical Medals 1760-1960, Volume 1: The Accession of George III to the Death of William IV*, Seaby, London, 1980.

C. E. Challis (ed.), *A New History of the Royal Mint*, Cambridge University Press, Cambridge, 1992.

Sir John Craig, *The Mint. A History of the London Mint from A.D. 287 to 1948*, Cambridge University Press, Cambridge, 1953.

R. Dalton and S. H. Hamer, *The Provincial Token-Coinage of the 18th Century Illustrated*, volumes 1-4, London, 1910-1915.

M. J. Daunton, *Progress and Poverty: An economic and Social History of Britain, 1700-1850*, Oxford University Press, Oxford, 1995.

Malcolm Dick (ed.), *Matthew Boulton (1728-1809): a Revolutionary Player*, Brewin, Studley, 2009.

G. P. Dyer, 'The Currency Crisis of 1797', *British Numismatic Journal*, 72, 2002, pp.135-142.

Henry W. Dickinson, *Matthew Boulton*, Cambridge University Press, Cambridge, 1937.

M. Dickinson, *Seventeenth Century Tokens of the British Isles and their Values*, London, 1986.

Richard Doty, *The Soho Mint and the Industrialization of Money*, British Numismatic Society Special Publication No 2, London, 1998.

D. W. Dykes, *Eighteenth Century Provincial Coinage [forthcoming]*.

Christopher Eimer, *British Commemorative Medals and their Values*, Seaby, London, 1987.

R. H. Elias and E. D. Finch (eds.), *Letters of Thomas Attwood Digges (1742-1821)*, Columbia, South Carolina, 1982.

L. Forrer, *Biographical Dictionary of Medallists*, Spink, London, 1904-1916.

Kenneth Garlick and Angus Macintyre (eds.), *The Diary of Joseph Farington, Vol. IV,* Yale University Press, New Haven and London, 1979.

Nicholas Goodison, *Matthew Boulton Ormolu*, Christies, London, 2002.

Nicholas Goodison, *Matthew Boulton's Trafalgar Medal*, Birmingham Museum and Art Gallery, Birmingham, 2007.

B. M. Gould, 'Matthew Boulton's East India Mint in London 1786-88', *Coin and Medal Bulletin*, No 612, 1969, pp.270-277.

C. R. Hawker, *Druid Tokens: Eighteenth century Token notes from Matthew Boulton's letters*, Brewin, Studley, 1996.

Peter M. Jones, *Industrial Enlightenment: Science, technology and culture in Birmingham and the West Midlands, 1760-1820*, Manchester University Press, Manchester, 2008.

Desmond King-Hele (ed.), *The Collected Letters of Erasmus Darwin*, Cambridge University Press, Cambridge, 2007.

H. E. Manville, *Tokens of the Industrial Revolution: Foreign Silver Coins Countermarked for Use in Great Britain c. 1787-1828*, British Numismatic Society Special Publication No. 3, Spink, London, 2001.

Richard Margolis, 'Matthew Boulton's French Ventures of 1791 and 1792: Tokens for the Monneron Frères of Paris', *British Numismatic Journal*, Vol. 58, 1988, pp.102-109.

Richard Margolis, 'Those Pests of Canals: A theft of Monneron tokens intended for France', *British Numismatic Journal*, Vol. 75, 2005, pp.121-131.

Shena Mason, *The Hardware Man's Daughter: Matthew Boulton and his 'Dear Girl'*, Phillimore, Chichester, 2005.

Shena Mason (ed.), *Matthew Boulton: 'Selling What All The World Desires'*, Yale University Press, London and New Haven, 2009.

Peter Matthias, *English Trade Tokens: The Industrial Revolution Illustrated*, Abelard-Schuma, London, 1962.

K. Morgan (ed.), *An American Quaker in the British Isles: the Travel Journal of Jabez, Maude Fisher, 1775-1779*, Oxford University Press, Oxford, 1992.

C. W. Peck, *Copper Coins of George III from English Copper, Tin and Bronze Coins in the British Museum 1558-1958*, British Museum, London, 1970.

J. G. Pollard, 'Matthew Boulton and J.P Droz', *The Numismatic Chronicle*, Vol. 8, 1968, pp.241-265.

J. G. Pollard, 'Matthew Boulton and Conrad Heinrich Küchler', *The Numismatic Chronicle*, Vol. 10, 1970, pp.259-318.

J. G Pollard, 'Matthew Boulton and the Reducing Machine in England', *The Numismatic Chronicle*, Vol. 11, 1971, pp.311-317.

F. Pridmore, *The Coins of the British Commonwealth of Nations to the end of the Reign of George VI, Part 2: Asian Territories*, Spink and Son, London, 1962.

F. Pridmore, *The Coins of the British Commonwealth of Nations to the end of the Reign of George VI, Part 3: Bermuda, British Guiana, British Honduras and the British West Indies*, Spink and Son, London, 1965.

F. Pridmore, *The Coins of the British Commonwealth of Nations to the end of the Reign of George VI, Part 4, India: Volume 1 East India Company Presidency Series c 1642-1835*, Spink and Son, London, 1975.

Charles Pye, *Provincial Copper Coins or Tokens issued between the Years 1787 and 1796*, Pearson, Birmingham, 1801.

Sir Eric Roll, *An Early Experiment in Industrial Organisation: Being a History of the Firm of Boulton and Watt 1775-1805*, Longmans, London, 1930; reprinted Cass, London, 1968.

George Selgin, 'Steam, Hot Air and Small Change: Matthew Boulton and the Reform of Britain's Coinage', *Economic History Review*, vol. LVI (3), 2003.

George Selgin, *Good Money. Birmingham Button Makers, the Royal Mint, and the Beginnings of Modern Coinage 1775-1821: Private Enterprise and Popular Coinage*, University of Michigan, Ann Arbor, 2008.

Stebbing Shaw, *The History and Antiquities of Staffordshire*, London, 1801.

Samuel Smiles, *Lives of Boulton and Watt*, John Murray, London, 1865.

R. Trogan and P. Sorel, *Augustin Dupré (1748-1833): médailleur et graveur général des monnaies de France*, Musée Carnavalet, Paris, 2000.

Wayne Turner, 'Wilkinson's trade tokens', *The Wilkinson Journal*, no. 7, 1979.

Chris Upton, *A History of Birmingham*, Phillimore, Chichester, 1997.

David Vice, 'A trial strike of a Birmingham counterfeiters die', *Format*, no. 37, 1988.

David Vice, *A Numismatic History of Soho Manufactory and Soho Mint 1772-1850*, British Numismatic Society Special Publication, London, forthcoming.

Arthur W. Waters, *Notes on Eighteenth Century Tokens*, Seaby, London, 1954.

Paul Withers, *Catalogue of the Collection of Coins, Medals, Medallions, Tokens, Dies etc. in the Assay Office Birmingham*, The Birmingham Assay Office, Birmingham, 1985.